Cornering Creative Writing

Learning Centers,
Games, Activities, and
Ideas for the
Elementary Classroom

INK

Written by
Imogene Forte,
Mary Ann Pangle, & Robbie Tupa

Other Kids' Stuff books:

Center Stuff for Nooks, Crannies and Corners
Complete Learning Centers for the Elementary Classroom
Imogene Forte, Mary Ann Pangle and Robbie Tupa

Creative Math Experiences for the Young Child
Imogene Forte and Joy MacKenzie

Creative Science Experiences for the Young Child
Imogene Forte and Joy MacKenzie

Kids' Stuff, Kindergarten and Nursery School
Mary Jo Collier, Imogene Forte and Joy MacKenzie

Kids' Stuff, L. P. Activity Record with Guide for
Teachers and Parents

Kids' Stuff, Reading and Language Experiences,
Intermediate – Jr. High
Imogene Forte, Marge Frank and Joy MacKenzie

Kids' Stuff, Reading and Spelling, Primary Level
Mary Jo Collier, Imogene Forte and Joy MacKenzie

Nooks, Crannies and Corners
Learning Centers for Creative Classrooms
Imogene Forte and Joy MacKenzie

Published by – Incentive Publications
Box 12522
Nashville, Tennessee 37212

Prologue

Once upon a time...

We vowed to find ways and means to encourage
students in our classrooms to write more
creatively, more spontaneously, and more often.

As a first step we took time out for a good clear
look at what we know about kids, about teaching
and learning, and about the creative process.

Next, we took a searching look at the environment
of our own classrooms. We tried to assess its
influence on student motivation and capacity for
creative thinking and writing.

Our third step was to develop the plans for "Setting
the Stage for Creative Writing" and the "Fifty-Two
Learning Centers". To enhance the effectiveness
of these centers in our classrooms we devised the
"Thirteen Games" to strengthen basic writing
skills and compiled the list of "Teacher Tactics"
to encourage young writers.

And now that we are experiencing the joy and
satisfaction that creative writing brings to students
and teachers we feel we have something worth
sharing. So here it is!

Imogene Forte
Mary Ann Pangle
Robbie Tupa

March, 1974

INCENTIVE PUBLICATIONS, Inc.

P.O. Box 12522
NASHVILLE, TENNESSEE 37212

TABLE OF CONTENTS

PART THREE - GAMESMANSHIP

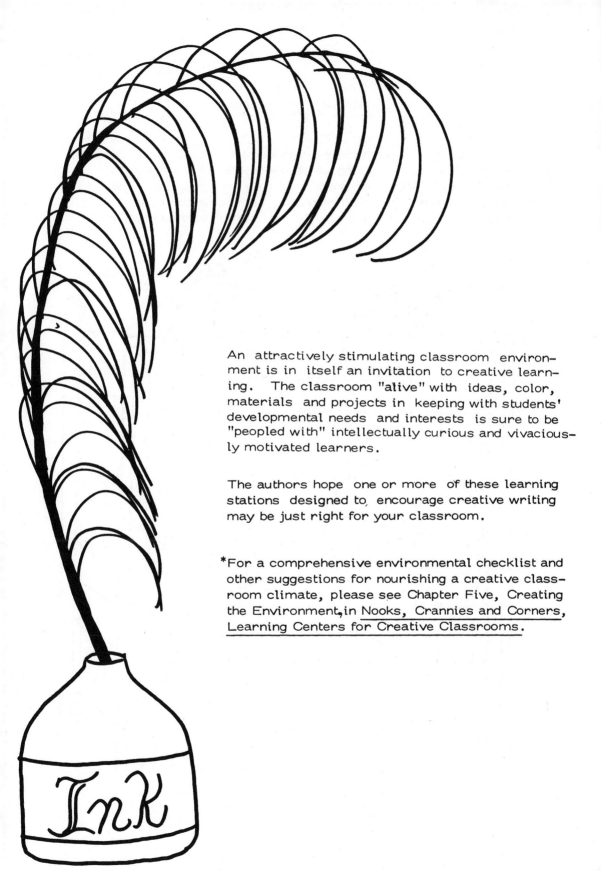

An attractively stimulating classroom environment is in itself an invitation to creative learning. The classroom "alive" with ideas, color, materials and projects in keeping with students' developmental needs and interests is sure to be "peopled with" intellectually curious and vivaciously motivated learners.

The authors hope one or more of these learning stations designed to encourage creative writing may be just right for your classroom.

*For a comprehensive environmental checklist and other suggestions for nourishing a creative classroom climate, please see Chapter Five, Creating the Environment, in Nooks, Crannies and Corners, Learning Centers for Creative Classrooms.

AUTHOR'S ATTIC

Utilize bunk beds from the salvage store to create a real feel of "specialness" for young writers who choose to retreat to the "Author's Attic" for privacy as they wax creative. The lower bed might contain idea books, anthologies or other materials to be used to motivate the "climb" to the creative level.

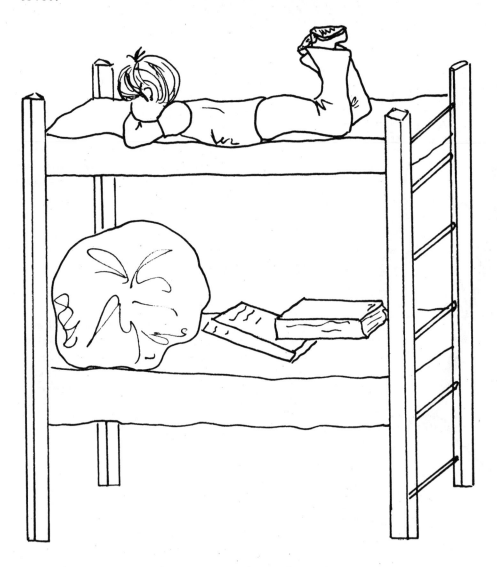

Book Bindery

Step 1
1. Trim the edges.
2. Sew the binding.

Step 2
1. Cut cardboard
2. Cover it with material.

Step 3
1. Using dry mount, iron the book to the cover.

BOOK BINDERY

A long table labeled "Book Bindery" can hold all the materials necessary for "binding" student-authored books. Encouraging students to make full use of these materials to attractively bind their books to be added to the classroom library will provide motivation for increased writing, and afford a great deal of satisfaction to the young authors.

CLASSROOM PRODUCTIONS, INC.

Standard classroom equipment may be rearranged to form a nook appropriate for use as the studio setting to motivate the writing of plays, television and radio commercials, and scripts and operettas. When actors, producers, and directors are selected, and the original works are actually produced, this activity becomes meaningful in a very real sense.

EDITOR'S DESK

Students will react positively to having their creative writing
checked by classmates when it is done at the "Editor's Desk"
as preparation for publication in the class newspaper, anthology
or magazine. Editors may be elected by popular vote to serve
for a given term. Equipment for the editor's desk will include
a good dictionary, a language rules book, red pencils, and paper
for writing correction and suggestion notes to the authors.

FICTION FORT

A simply built wooden
fort reached by means
of a wooden stairway,
strategically placed
just outside the class-
room, could inspire
many "tall tales" of
the old West or the
brave new frontier.

ILLUSTRATORS LIMITED

A table, chairs, and a couple of easels will be all the equipment needed to furnish the classroom "studio" for illustrators of creative masterpieces.

A variety of paper, poster board, paints, pencils, crayons, magic markers, paste, scissors, fabric pieces, ribbon, buttons, laces, yarns, and other scrap basket goodies will motivate continued creative thinking as students select the media and form for their illustrations.

POETS' CORNER

Two bean bag chairs and a small table can be used to transform a quiet corner of the classroom into a poets' corner.

On the table place

> ...a 3 x 5" file box containing index
> cards with suggested titles for poems
> ...a box containing lists of rhyming
> words
> ...work sheets with first lines of haiku
> and cinquain
> ...pads and pencils
> ...a dictionary
> ...several good poetry anthologies
> ...a looseleaf notebook attractively covered
> to hold completed poems

POSTMAN'S HOLIDAY

A large mailbox, made from a corrugated cardboard box covered with construction paper or painted with tempera can be utilized for distribution of letters written by members of the class to the teacher or to classmates. A postman can be elected by the class and a special time set aside for delivering letters.

Letters from the teacher will be especially welcome and will provide an excellent avenue for very personal teacher–pupil communication.

Rules for letter writing and suggestions for making letters interesting may be printed on charts and displayed near the mailbox.

PRESS CLUB

A classroom "press club" where authors and would-be authors can go to discuss and critique their work with others is a definite plus for teachers wishing to motivate their students to write more creatively. Bookcases or desks may be rearranged for this purpose or a coat or storage room might be utilized.

Sh-h-h
I'm thinking...

PRIVACY REQUESTED

In classrooms short on
"corner" space, a table,
chairs and a tri—fold
plywood screen may be
utilized to create a private
place to accommodate
student writers' needs.

REPORTERS' SAFARI

A tent made of a blanket spread between chairs and decorated
with a jungle motif will encourage young writers to add to a
collection of animal stories compiled by the class. This
collection could be bound into an anthology to be presented
to students in another classroom.

This activity might serve as a colminating project for a
Social Studies or Science unit.

RIDDLE ROCKET

The back of the piano or
teacher's desk or an unused wall
space may become the "launching
pad" for a large rocket made from
tagboard and labeled "riddle
rocket". A table near the rocket
containing riddle books, pencils and
strips of tagboard will enable
students to print original riddles
to be pinned on the rocket. Each
riddle may be numbered to
correspond to a tagboard answer
strip to be prepared and placed
in the "answer unit" to enable
"guessers" to check their answers.

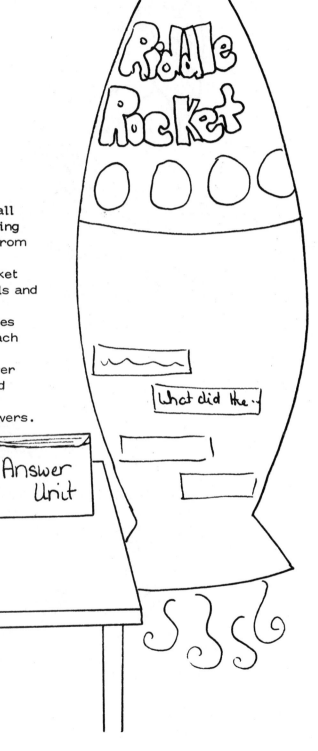

TITLES AHOY

A small unused sailboat or canoe can be easily converted to a writer's nook. This could be especially attractive to students if incorporated in a unit on the sea, lakes or rivers.

TRAVEL AGENCY

Post colorful travel posters around the walls behind a table holding travel folders, magazines, maps, encyclopedias and resource books. Provide time for students to work in this center to create travel brochures, articles for travel magazines, newspaper columns or stories dealing with places of interest to them. Research related to clothes and equipment for the trip, time and method of travel, cost, type of housing, food and recreation available will add interest to this project. Students will enjoy "selling" their trip to classmates.

UNDER THE MAGIC UMBRELLA

A colorful umbrella hung from the ceiling over
a round rug holding fat cushions and pads and
pencils may provide just the "magic spot" to
inspire students to write fanciful stories and
poetry.

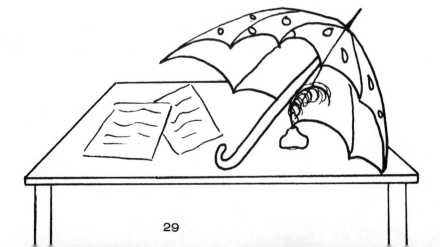

WRITERS' HIDEAWAY

A refrigerator or deep freeze box, attractively decorated and labeled "Writers' Hideaway" may be used by the student who feels he needs complete privacy in which to write his science fiction or black magic story. A beach towel or blanket spread on the floor, a dictionary, and pads and pencils will serve to expedite the author's purpose. The sides of the box might be used for displaying stories or poems completed here. To make this a "special" project, the hideaway might sometimes be designated for exclusive use of students interested in writing about the specifically designated topic, such as "The Pirate's Treasure", "The Land of Giants", "An Unnamed Planet", "A Lost Ship", Fogbound", "In Lollipop Land", etc.

Notes

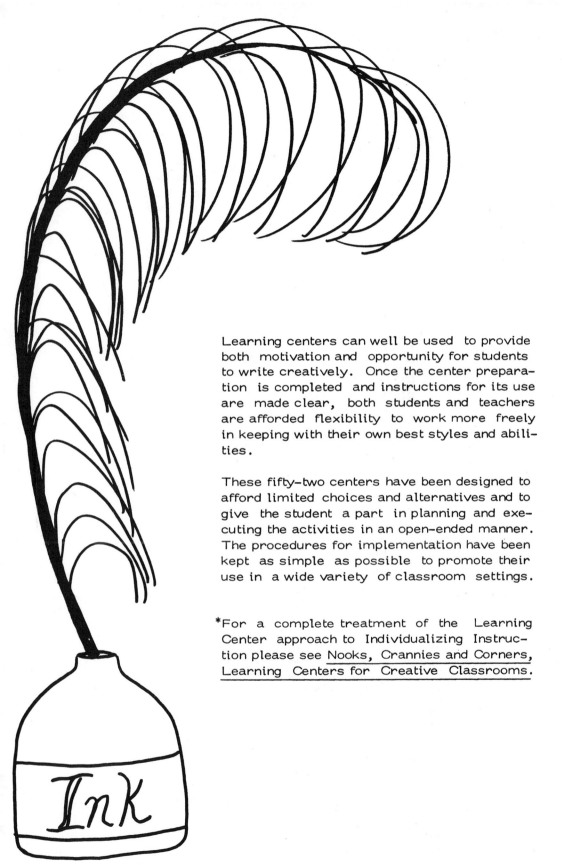

Learning centers can well be used to provide both motivation and opportunity for students to write creatively. Once the center preparation is completed and instructions for its use are made clear, both students and teachers are afforded flexibility to work more freely in keeping with their own best styles and abilities.

These fifty-two centers have been designed to afford limited choices and alternatives and to give the student a part in planning and executing the activities in an open-ended manner. The procedures for implementation have been kept as simple as possible to promote their use in a wide variety of classroom settings.

*For a complete treatment of the Learning Center approach to Individualizing Instruction please see Nooks, Crannies and Corners, Learning Centers for Creative Classrooms.

All Gone

PURPOSE:

After completing this center, the student should be able to write a solution to a possible life crisis brought about by a resource shortage.

CENTER PREPARATION:

Arrange the center attractively. As a focal point make a large gasoline pump and label it "Empty".

ALL GONE

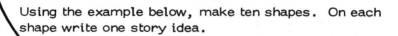

Using the example below, make ten shapes. On each shape write one story idea.

Very
little
gasoline
available
–
no vacation

School during summer vacation –
   no heat during the winter
Paper shortage – no homework
No television – low on electricity
Can't take a bath – little water
Mothers upset – no make–up
Must wear best pants – no cotton
   to make jeans
No bread – a hamburger without a
   bun?
Toy shops going out of business – no
   plastic

On a bulletin board, place the gasoline pump and shapes.

PROCEDURE FOR IMPLEMENTATION:

1.   Introduce the center through a discussion of possible
     resource shortages that might affect our daily lives.

2.   Instruct students to select an idea to use in a story.
     Ask them to tell how the crisis could affect their lives
     and to suggest a solution.

3.   Provide time for students to write additional stories.

4.   Make provision for sharing, displaying, or filing
     the completed stories.

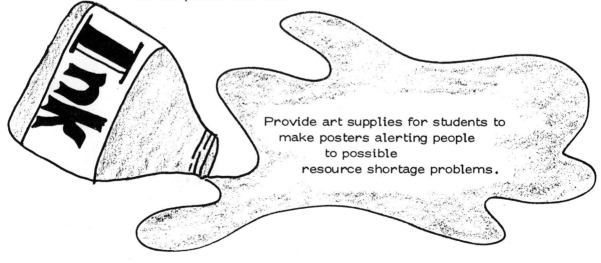

Provide art supplies for students to
make posters alerting people
to possible
resource shortage problems.

Believe It Or Not

PURPOSE:

> After completing this center, the student should
> be able to creatively write a myth.

CENTER PREPARATION:

To motivate the students, mount animal pictures
in the center. Under each animal print the myth
ideas.

How did the turtle get
his shell?

How did the giraffe
get his long neck?

How did the lion get
his roar?

How did the rabbit get
his fluffy tail?

How did the elephant get his
trunk?

BELIEVE IT OR NOT

 How did the cat get his meow?

How did the kangaroo get his pocket?

How did the skunk get his smell?

How did the reindeer get his antlers?

How did the bird get its song?

PROCEDURE FOR IMPLEMENTATION:

1. Introduce the center by reading and discussing a myth.

2. Instruct students to select an idea and write a myth.

3. Make provision for sharing, displaying, or filing myths.

Provide art supplies for students to draw a picture of the animal before it became what it is today.

36

Bon Voyage

PURPOSE:

After completing this center, the student should be able to take an imaginary trip and write a creative story.

CENTER PREPARATION:

To motivate students, place a suitcase on the creative writing table. Using colored paper, make travel stickers. On each travel sticker, print one idea:

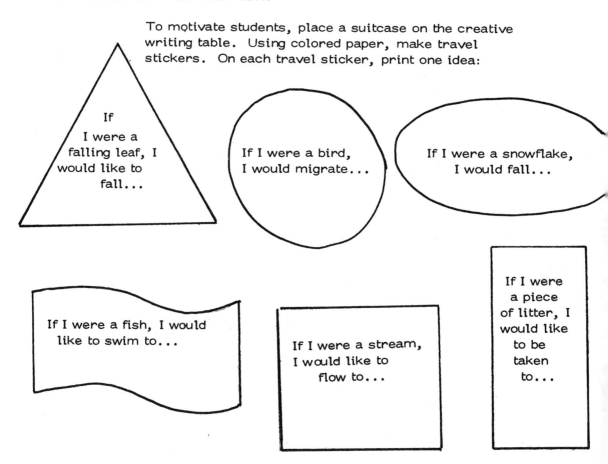

If I were a falling leaf, I would like to fall...

If I were a bird, I would migrate...

If I were a snowflake, I would fall...

If I were a fish, I would like to swim to...

If I were a stream, I would like to flow to...

If I were a piece of litter, I would like to be taken to...

BON VOYAGE

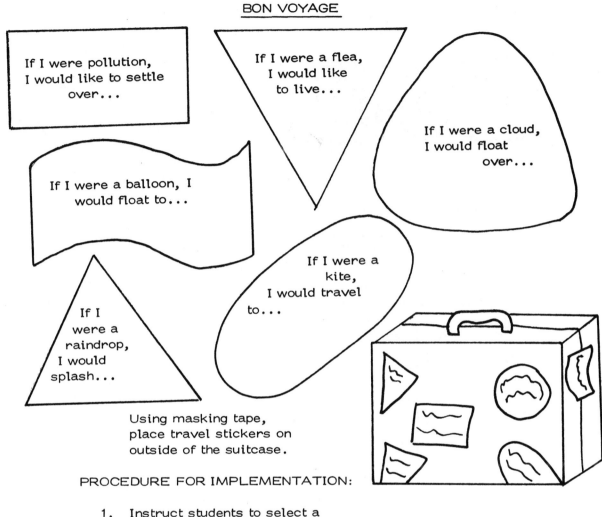

If I were pollution, I would like to settle over...

If I were a flea, I would like to live...

If I were a cloud, I would float over...

If I were a balloon, I would float to...

If I were a kite, I would travel to...

If I were a raindrop, I would splash...

Using masking tape, place travel stickers on outside of the suitcase.

PROCEDURE FOR IMPLEMENTATION:

1. Instruct students to select a travel sticker and write a story.

2. Provide time for students to write additional stories.

3. Make provision for sharing, displaying, or filing their Bon Voyage stories.

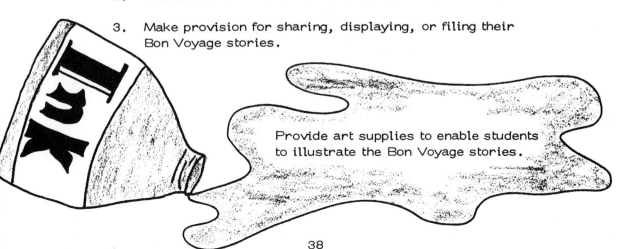

Provide art supplies to enable students to illustrate the Bon Voyage stories.

PURPOSE:

> After completing this center, the student should
> be able to write creative programs for television.

CENTER PREPARATION:

Arrange the center attractively. As a focal point,
make a picture of a television set.

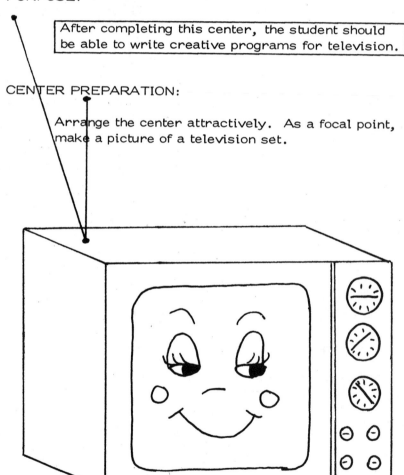

BOOB TUBE

PROCEDURE FOR IMPLEMENTATION:

1. To introduce the center take a poll of favorite
    television programs. Use the poll results as a
    discussion topic to stimulate interest in the center.

2. Instruct students to create a script for a new
    television program.

3. After the script has been evaluated, the programs
    can be taped.

4. Make a television set by using a cardboard box.
    Cut out one side for a screen. Insert two dowels
    to be used as rollers. Provide a roll of shelf paper
    for students to illustrate their program. When
    drawings are completed, mount the shelf paper on
    the dowels.

5. Provide a time for students to view the newly created
    television programs and to listen to the accompanying
    script.

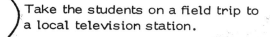

Take the students on a field trip to
a local television station.

Candy Couplets

PURPOSE:

> After completing this center, the student should be able to develop an awareness of poetry and to write couplets.

CENTER PREPARATION:

Arrange the center attractively. As a focal point for the center make a Candy Couplet Tree using a tree branch in a weighted can.

Print couplet ideas on strips of paper and attach a piece of wrapped candy to each idea. To the branch of the tree, tie the candy couplet idea.

41

CANDY COUPLETS

Candy Couplet ideas:

rainbow	mouse	school	home	flower
dragon	lion	friend	desk	love
rain	dog	ball	boat	peace
happy	sad	cry	sick	ground
dirt	Mars	train	town	teacher

PROCEDURE FOR IMPLEMENTATION:

1. Introduce the center by reading couplets.

2. Instruct students to pick a Candy Couplet idea and write a creative couplet. After completing the couplet, the student may eat the candy.

3. Encourage students to use their own ideas to write additional couplets.

4. Make provision for sharing, displaying, or filing Candy Couplets.

Provide art supplies so students can illustrate their couplets.

Chicken Chatter

PURPOSE:

After completing this center, the student should
be able to creatively write a dialogue.

CENTER PREPARATION:

As a focal point of the center, enlarge the picture
above. Mount it on the bulletin board to motivate
students. Collect eleven plastic eggs that can be
opened. Print the dialogue ideas on individual strips
of paper and put one idea inside each egg. Place
the eggs in a basket.

Dialogue ideas:

What would a bar of soap
say to dirty hands?

What might lightning
say to thunder?

What would one library
book say to another library
book?

What might a tricycle say to
a bicycle when the owner
was too big to ride the
tricycle?

What would a goldfish and
a guppie together in a fish
bowl say to each other?

43

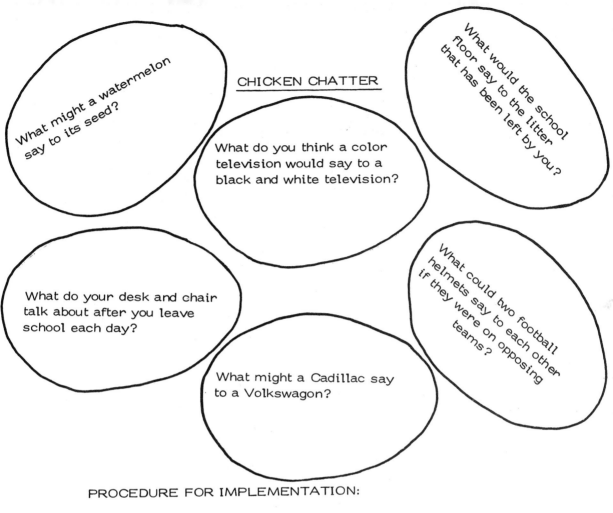

CHICKEN CHATTER

What might a watermelon say to its seed?

What do you think a color television would say to a black and white television?

What would the school floor say to the litter that has been left by you?

What do your desk and chair talk about after you leave school each day?

What might a Cadillac say to a Volkswagon?

What could two football helmets say to each other if they were on opposing teams?

PROCEDURE FOR IMPLEMENTATION:

1. Introduce the center by reviewing quotation marks and their use in written dialogue.

2. Instruct students to take an egg, open it, and from the idea write a creative dialogue.

3. Encourage students to write additional stories.

4. Make provision for sharing, displaying, or filing completed stories.

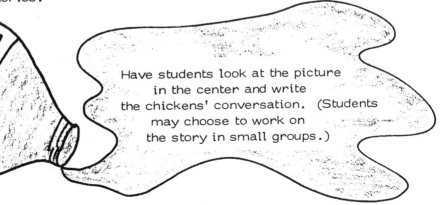

Have students look at the picture in the center and write the chickens' conversation. (Students may choose to work on the story in small groups.)

Circus Craze

PURPOSE:

After completing this center, the student should be able to express himself creatively by writing a story.

CENTER PREPARATION:

Draw a clown and place on the bulletin board in the center. Make eight balloons using tagboard and tempera paints. Print one circus adventure on each balloon. Attach string from each mounted balloon to the clown's hand.

Circus adventures:

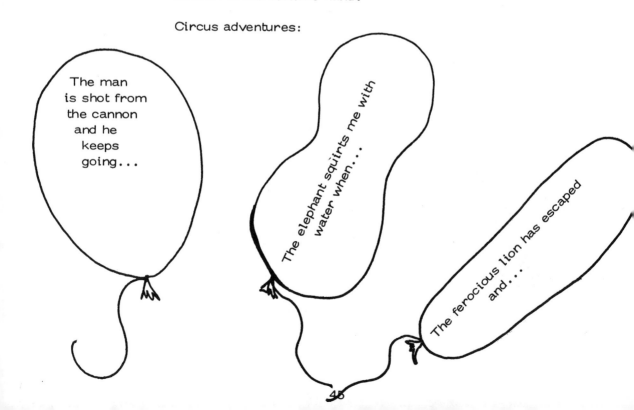

The man is shot from the cannon and he keeps going...

The elephant squirts me with water when...

The ferocious lion has escaped and...

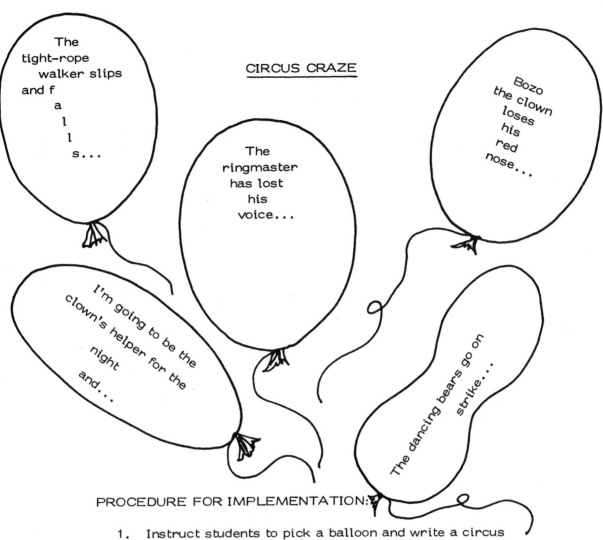

CIRCUS CRAZE

The tight-rope walker slips and f a l l s...

The ringmaster has lost his voice...

Bozo the clown loses his red nose...

I'm going to be the clown's helper for the night and...

The dancing bears go on strike...

PROCEDURE FOR IMPLEMENTATION:

1. Instruct students to pick a balloon and write a circus adventure story.

2. Make provision for sharing, displaying, or filing circus adventures.

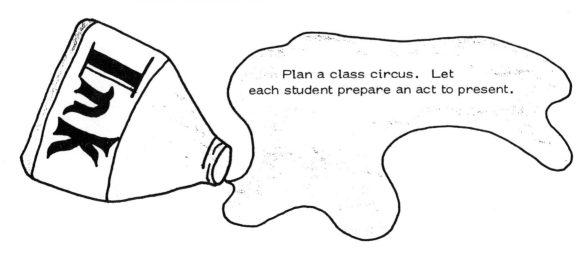

INK

Plan a class circus. Let each student prepare an act to present.

Color Splash

PURPOSE:

After completing this center, the student should
be able to interpret and creatively express colors
and their usage.

CENTER PREPARATION:

Arrange the center attractively. Using different
colors of construction paper, cut shapes. Print
one color idea on each shape.

Why are fire engines red?

Why do baby boys wear blue?

Why do baby girls wear pink?

Why do nurses wear white?

Why do policemen wear blue?

COLOR SPLASH

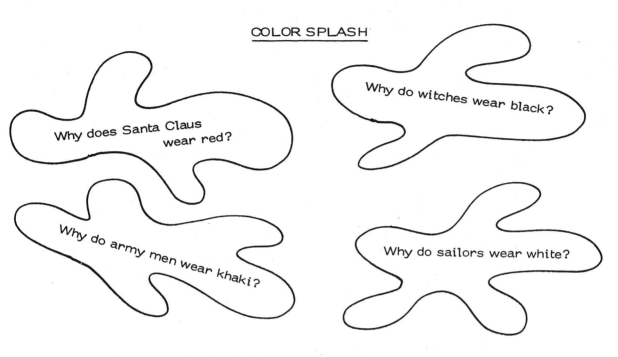

Why does Santa Claus wear red?

Why do witches wear black?

Why do army men wear khaki?

Why do sailors wear white?

PROCEDURE FOR IMPLEMENTATION:

1. Instruct students to select a color idea and write a creative story.

2. Inside a brightly decorated box, put the following ideas:

    1. Why is the sun yellow?   5. Why is grass green?
    2. Why is the sky blue?   6. Why is snow white?
    3. Why is water clear?   7. Why are leaves green?
    4. Why is the ocean blue?   8. Why is a rainbow many colors?

3. Provide resource books and allow additional time for students to pursue these ideas and write a paragraph or a story.

4. Make provision for sharing, displaying or filing color stories.

Ink

Provide art supplies. On a card list the following colors: red, yellow, blue, green, orange, purple, black. Instruct students to select a color and draw a picture showing how this color affects them.

Comic Carnival

PURPOSE:

> After completing this center, the student should be able to create his own cartoon characters and develop a comic strip.

CENTER PREPARATION:

> To provide background for the center, mount Sunday comic strips on a bulletin board.

COMIC CARNIVAL

PROCEDURE FOR IMPLEMENTATION:

1. Introduce the center by leading a discussion of comic strip characters. Culminate the discussion by helping students develop three imaginary characters. Instruct students to use the three imaginary characters to develop a class comic strip. Ask them to plan and work together so that each person will be responsible for one section of the comic strip. Provide drawing paper and crayons for the completion of this activity.

2. For another center activity instruct students to develop a comic strip for a large newspaper for a one-week period. Provide chart tablet paper and crayons for each student.

3. Just for fun, the students might enjoy devising a comic strip with their teacher as the main character.

4. Make provisions for sharing, displaying or filing comic strips.

Provide paper for the students to draw them-selves as famous cartoonists.

Commercial Rehearsal

PURPOSE:

> After completing this center, the student should be able to create a song or a poem that advertises a newly developed product.

CENTER PREPARATION:

Arrange the center to stimulate interest in advertising.

Using tempera paint and tagboard, the following products could be enlarged to be mounted on the bulletin board.

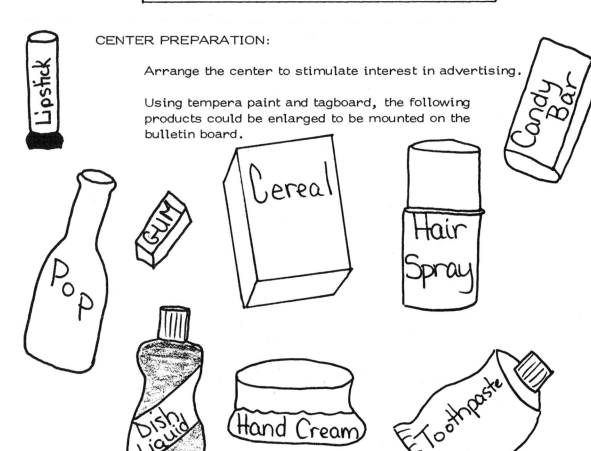

COMMERCIAL REHEARSAL

PROCEDURE FOR IMPLEMENTATION:

1. Introduce the center to the group with a discussion of various types of advertising.

2. Provide time for students to listen to radio commercials.

3. Instruct students to select a product from the bulletin board, name the product, and then write a song or a poem to advertise it.

4. Encourage originality by asking students to create a new product. An example of this might be:

A poem or a song is to be written to advertise the newly created product.

5. Make provision for sharing, displaying, or filing the commercial.

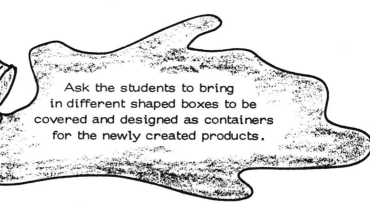

Ask the students to bring in different shaped boxes to be covered and designed as containers for the newly created products.

Cooking Contest

PURPOSE:

> After completing this center, the student should
> be able to express himself more creatively.

CENTER PREPARATION:

Make a picture of two children
cooking. Place the picture in
the center to help motivate the
students. Write the recipe
ideas on index cards and place
them in a recipe box.

Recipe ideas:

1. 2 strawberries
    1 bad boy
    1 tennis shoe

2. 1 banana peel
    1 coat hanger
    2 stones

3. 1/2 popsicle
    1 cold day
    3 white mice

4. 3/4 apple pie
    1 deserted lake
    1 policeman

5. 1/2 watermelon
    1 smokestack
    3 earrings

6. 1 quart milk
    1 frog
    1/2 basement

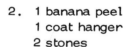

COOKING CONTEST

7. 2 steaks
   1 lipstick
   1 party

8. 1 ice cream cone
   2 toadstools
   1 telephone

9. 1/2 hamburger
   1 witch
   1 radio

10. 2 lollipops
    1 ruler
    1 Volkswagen

PROCEDURE FOR IMPLEMENTATION:

1. Prepare directions that instruct the student to look in the recipe box and select a recipe they would like to "cook up". The student is to write a story including all the ingredients.

2. Make provision for sharing, displaying, or filing the story recipes.

Provide drawing paper, crayons, and scissors to enable students to draw their cooking creations. Have a cooking contest and display the pictures. Award prizes.

Doodle Bug

PURPOSE:

> After completing this center, the student should
> be able to select a symbol to use as a focal point
> for writing a creative story.

CENTER PREPARATION:

Arrange the center attractively. As a focal point
for the center, make a large bug using tagboard
and paints. Draw "doodle" symbols on squares of
tagboard.

DOODLE BUG

Place in the center the following "doodle" classification code:

```
                         Doodle Code

    happy        careful     cool            wild
    serious      fussy       tempermental    irresistible
    successful   tough       gross           interesting
    sad          blah        busy            spooky
```

PROCEDURE FOR IMPLEMENTATION:

1. Instruct students to select an unusual "doodle" and write a story adventure.

2. Provide additional time so students can create their own "doodle" and write another story.

3. Let students draw a "doodle" that matches the "doodle" code word that has been placed in the center.

4. Make provision for sharing, displaying, or filing "doodles" and stories.

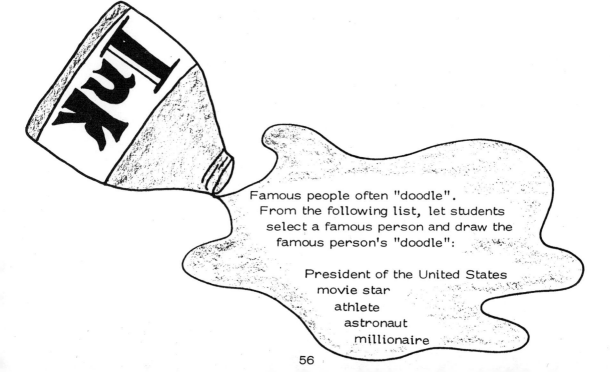

Famous people often "doodle".
From the following list, let students select a famous person and draw the famous person's "doodle":

President of the United States
movie star
athlete
astronaut
millionaire

PURPOSE:

After completing this center, the student should be able to write a story describing the requirements of an imaginary occupation.

CENTER PREPARATION:

Using tagboard and tempera paints make a picture of the moon. Attach a sign "Jobs Available". Mount the picture and sign on a bulletin board backed with black construction paper.

EMPLOYMENT AGENCY

Using manila drawing paper, prepare a newspaper entitled "Moon Gazette". In the classified pages, list the following available jobs:

dust collector	weatherman
rock sorter	Rover mechanic
lamplighter	earth photographer
crater guide	oxygen supplier
moon cook	footprint detective
moon phone operator	landing and takeoff specialist
	traffic cop

Arrange the center attractively and place a newspaper in it.

PROCEDURE FOR IMPLEMENTATION:

1. Instruct students to select a want ad from tne newspaper and write a story describing the imaginary moon occupation and the qualifications required for the job.

2. Provide necessary art supplies for students to design an appropriate application form. After completing the applications, students in the center may decide who is best qualified for the moon occupations.

3. Make provision for sharing, displaying or filing the completed activities.

Provide art supplies for students to illustrate themselves in their new jobs. The pictures may be cut and mounted on the center bulletin board.

PURPOSE:

> After completing this center, the student should
> be able to write a fable.

CENTER PREPARATION:

Arrange the center attractively using animal
pictures.

FABLE FROLIC

In the center, provide books of fables. Print the
following directions on a piece of tagboard and
place in the center.

> Read a fable and answer the following questions:
>
> 1. What is the name of the fable?
> 2. Who are the main characters?
> 3. What is the moral?

PROCEDURE FOR IMPLEMENTATION:

1. Introduce the center by reading and discussing fables
   in a small group setting.

2. Instruct students to read a fable and answer the
   questions that have been placed in the center.

3. Students may then select two animals from the
   center to use as characters in a creative fable.

4. Allow the student to spend as much time in this
   center as he wishes.

5. Make provision for sharing, filing, or displaying fables.

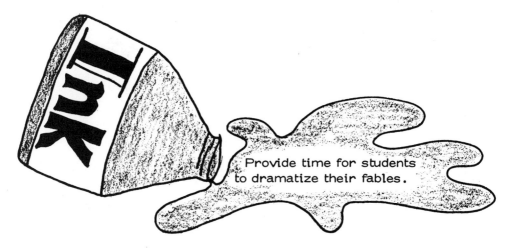

Provide time for students
to dramatize their fables.

Feeling Forecast

PURPOSE:

After completing this center, the student should
be able to express how their feelings are affected
by weather conditions.

CENTER PREPARATION:

Arrange the center with various weather symbols.
Using tagboard and tempera paint make a raindrop,
sun, snowflake, fluffy white cloud, dark cloud,
streak of lightning, and tornado symbols. On each
symbol print one weather phrase.

A

rainy day

makes me...

When there are fluffy white clouds

in the sky...

FEELING FORECAST

Sunny days make me feel...

When I see lightning, I...

I wake up and find snow and feel...

Dark stormy clouds make me...

A tornado watch makes me feel...

PROCEDURE FOR IMPLEMENTATION:

1. To set the climate for the center, read poetry about different kinds of weather.

2. Instruct students to select a weather symbol and write a paragraph expressing how this weather condition affects them.

3. Encourage students to write about several different weather conditions.

4. Make provision for sharing, displaying, or filing weather paragraphs.

Prepare a corner of the room and provide mural paper and art supplies. On the mural paint the weather symbols that are in the center. Instruct students to choose a weather symbol and draw themselves as they will look on this type of day.

INK

from Beginning to End

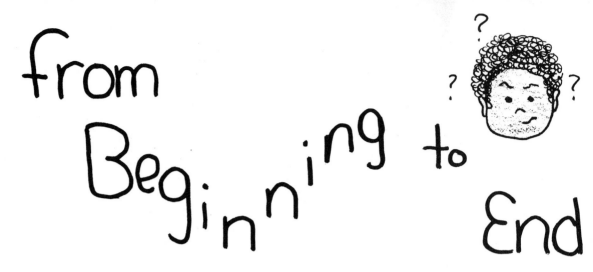

PURPOSE:

> After completing this center, the student should
> be able to develop and write a creative story
> when given a story ending.

CENTER PREPARATION:

Arrange the center attractively, using a maze made
from yarn as the focal point.

Print story endings on strips of tagboard and mount
in the middle of the maze.

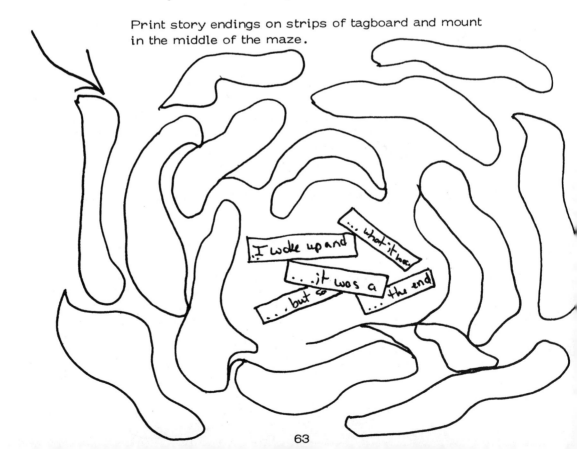

FROM BEGINNING TO END

Story Endings:

...they headed their spaceship toward earth.
...I woke up and found it was only a dream.
...I became myself again.
...the cowboys rode off in the distance.
...the terrifying week had finally ended.
...the winning run was scored.
...the magic spell was broken.
...the leprechan left as quietly as he had arrived.
...the tracks led nowhere.
...he laughed and then vanished.
...it was a success.
...they were dripping wet, but safe.

PROCEDURE FOR IMPLEMENTATION:

1. Instruct students to choose a story ending, develop the sequence of events, and write a complete story.

2. Make provision for sharing, displaying, or filing maze stories.

Provide art supplies for students to use to illustrate stories.

Gertrude's Gossip

PURPOSE:

> After completing this center, the student should be able to write a creative solution to an imaginary problem.

CENTER PREPARATION:

As a focal point of the center, enlarge the following newspaper pages:

Dear Gertrude,
     My mother won't let me eat candy before lunch. What should I do?

                              Sweet Tooth

Dear Gertrude,
     My teacher gives too much homework. I have no time to play. Help!

                              Fed Up

Dear Gertrude,
     I have to be in bed at 8:00 each night. My friends are allowed to stay up until 9:00. What's wrong with my parents?

                              Wide Awake

Dear Gertrude,
     Grandmother is coming and Mother says I must get my hair cut. How can I escape the scissors?

                              Shaggy

Dear Gertrude,
     My brother calls me "Shrimp". I hate that name. How can I make him stop?

                              Shortie

Dear Gertrude,
     I am planning to run away. Any suggestions?

                              Hobo

Dear Gertrude,
     How could I get Doug to notice me?

                              Cutie Pie

GERTRUDE'S GOSSIP

Dear Gertrude,
    I love desserts. Why won't Mother let me have two?

                                        Fattie

Dear Gertrude,
    The cost of living is going up! Fifty cents is not enough
for an allowance. What should I do?

                                        Broke

Dear Gertrude,
    I have to share a bedroom with my sister. How can I move
her out?

                                        Crowded

Dear Gertrude,
    My job is washing dishes every night. How can I change
jobs?

                                        Chapped Hands

Mount the newspaper in the center and arrange
attractively.

PROCEDURE FOR IMPLEMENTATION:

1. Instruct students to pretend they are Gertrude and
    write a solution to one of the problems.

2. Allow each student to spend as much time in this
    center as he wishes.

3. Make provision for sharing, displaying, or filing
    Gertrude's solutions.

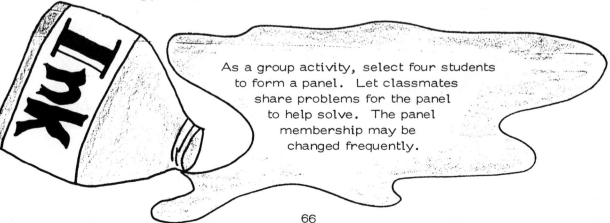

As a group activity, select four students
to form a panel. Let classmates
share problems for the panel
to help solve. The panel
membership may be
changed frequently.

Haiku Happenings

PURPOSE:

After completing this center, the student should be able to develop an awareness of poetry and be able to write haikus.

CENTER PREPARATION:

Using black paint and tagboard, enlarge the Japanese characters. Make a large paintbrush, and bottle of ink. Place in the center and arrange attractively.

HAIKU HAPPENINGS

PROCEDURE FOR IMPLEMENTATION:

1. Haiku is a three-line verse with a total of seventeen syllables. It usually does not rhyme. Haiku often suggests a thought or feeling about nature. Introduce the center with a discussion of haiku.

2. Instruct students to write a haiku using one of the following ideas:

the sea	a sunset	falling leaves
the wind	a flower	a mountain
raindrops	the moon	clouds

3. Additional time may be provided for students to create their own topics and haikus.

4. Make provision for sharing, displaying, or filing completed haikus.

Provide India ink and drawing paper for students to letter and illustrate their haiku.

PURPOSE:

> After completing this center, the student should
> be able to create a written solution when given
> a difficult situation.

CENTER PREPARATION:

Arrange the center attractively.

Make a large ten-page booklet. On each page
print one story situation.

1. Your rowboat springs a leak...

2. Swimming under water, you discover your air
    tank is empty...

3. An escaped circus lion is heading your way...

4. Traveling down the river, you are suddenly
    heading for a waterfall...

5. Speeding along the race track, your car runs
    out of gas...

6. You wake up to find a flashlight shining in your
    window...

7. While climbing a ladder you slip...

8. Playing in the woods, you become lost...

9. While exploring a cave, your light goes out...

10. I came face to face with a bear, while camping...

Make a cover for the booklet.

PROCEDURE FOR IMPLEMENTATION:

1. Instruct students to look through the book, choose a story situation, and write a story solution.

2. Make provision for sharing, displaying, or filing story solutions.

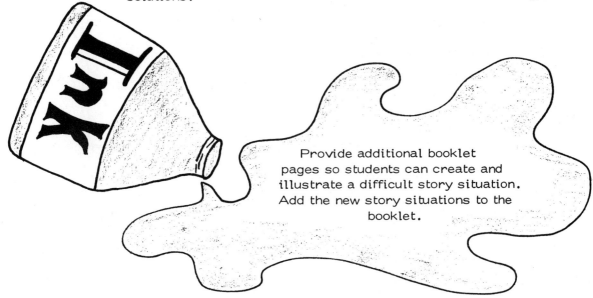

Provide additional booklet pages so students can create and illustrate a difficult story situation. Add the new story situations to the booklet.

Hold That Line

PURPOSE:

After completing this center, the student should be able to organize and creatively present written directions for playing a game.

CENTER PREPARATION:

Arrange the center attractively, using a picture of a football player as the focal point.

Print the following directions on a large chart:

1. Fold a 9" x 12" sheet of drawing paper.

2. Design the cover of the football rulebook.

3. On the inside, write the directions for a football game.

4. On the back, list the necessary equipment for the football game.

HOLD THAT LINE

PROCEDURE FOR IMPLEMENTATION:

1. Lead a group discussion related to games and the necessity for rules. Discuss what would happen in a football game if there were no rules.

2. Instruct students to follow the directions that are printed on the chart and write a rule book for football.

3. Provide time for students to write a rule book for a game that has never been invented.

4. Make provision for playing the new games.

Prepare a football field on the bulletin board. Students can draw the person they would most like to be at a football game and mount it on the bulletin board.

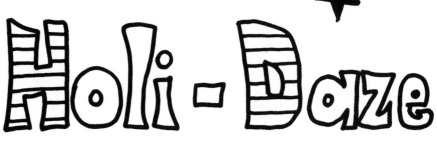

Holi - Daze

PURPOSE:

> After completing this center, the student should
> be able to create a new holiday and express
> creative ways to celebrate the holiday.

CENTER PREPARATION:

Make a collage of holiday materials to be used as
the focal point of the center.

HOLI-DAZE

PROCEDURE FOR IMPLEMENTATION:

1. Introduce the center by leading a discussion covering different holidays and the related customs. Instruct students to write a report on a holiday that is native to another country and tell how it is celebrated. Provide appropriate resource books and reference materials.

2. Prepare the following guide to help students create and write a story about a new holiday complete with its own traditions.

---

1. What is the name of the holiday?

2. When is the holiday celebrated?

3. Why is the holiday celebrated?

4. Who will celebrate the holiday?

5. What preparations will be needed?

6. What type of food will be provided?

7. Will this be a family, local or national holiday?

8. What will be the entertainment?

---

3. Make provisions for sharing, displaying, or filing holiday stories.

Prepare a table for an exhibit of holiday dioramas to be made from "scrap bag" materials.

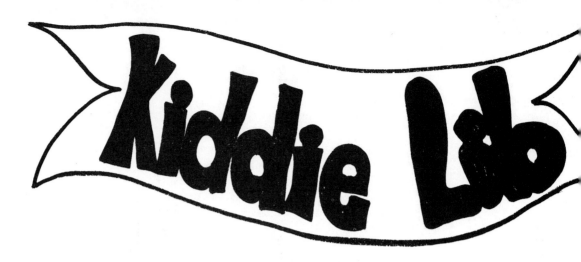

PURPOSE:

> After completing this center, the student should
> be able to express awareness of individual rights
> and responsibilities.

CENTER PREPARATION:

Arrange the center using a banner proclaiming
"Kiddie Lib Week".

Prepare the following center directions:

> During "Kiddie Lib Month" people under the age
> of fourteen will be given special privileges, more
> responsibility, and more independence. How will
> your role change as a member of your family and
> as a student in the classroom? Will this change
> any of your friendships? Write a story telling
> about your experiences during "Kiddie Lib Week".

KIDDIE LIB

PROCEDURE FOR IMPLEMENTATION:

1. As an introduction to the center, lead a group discussion dealing with individual rights and responsibilities of people living in a democracy.

2. Instruct students to read and follow the directions that have been placed in the center and write a story.

3. Encourage students to write additional stories.

4. Make provision for sharing, displaying, or filing "Kiddie Lib" stories.

19–	Month			19–	
	1	2	3	4	5
6	7	8	9	10	11	12
"Kiddie Lib Week"					
20	21	22	23	24	25	26
27	28	29	30	31		

Provide a time for students to dramatize some of their unique experiences that occurred during "Kiddie Lib" week.

PURPOSE:

After completing this center, the students should
be able to create puppet characters and to write
a puppet play.

CENTER PREPARATION:

Arrange the center attractively. On a table place
the following materials:

wooden spoons   glue   buttons
(kitchen or ice cream felt
  spoons)   material scraps
beads (jewelry)   construction
yarn   paper

Make a puppet to serve as a model. For a puppet
stage use a table, desk, movable bulletin board,
chair, or cardboard box.

KNOCK ON WOOD

Prepare the following list of settings for a puppet play:

city	home	car	wild west
tree house	school	forest	zoo
store	castle	farm	moon
foreign country	hospital	circus	battle field
ocean bottom	space ship	cave	submarine

Provide art supplies for students to draw background scenery.

PROCEDURE FOR IMPLEMENTATION:

1. Instruct students to choose a setting and write a puppet play.

2. After the play has been written, ask them to make wooden spoon puppets to represent two characters in the play.

3. Using the art supplies, make background scenery.

4. Provide time for students to present puppet plays to their classmates.

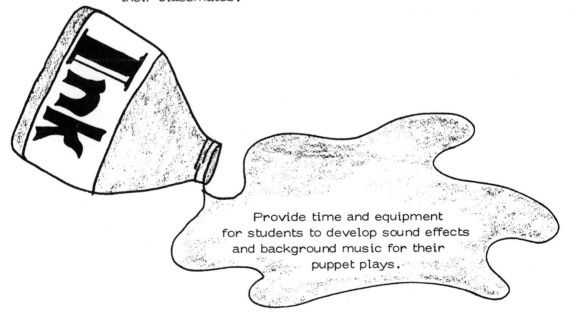

Provide time and equipment for students to develop sound effects and background music for their puppet plays.

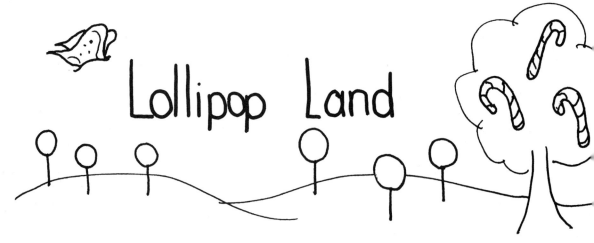

Lollipop Land

PURPOSE:

After completing this center, the student should
be able to write a creative story.

CENTER PREPARATION:

Arrange the center attractively. As a focal
point for the center, make nine lollipops using
tagboard and tempera paints. Print one story
idea on each lollipop. Cut and mount the lollipops
in the center.

Story ideas:

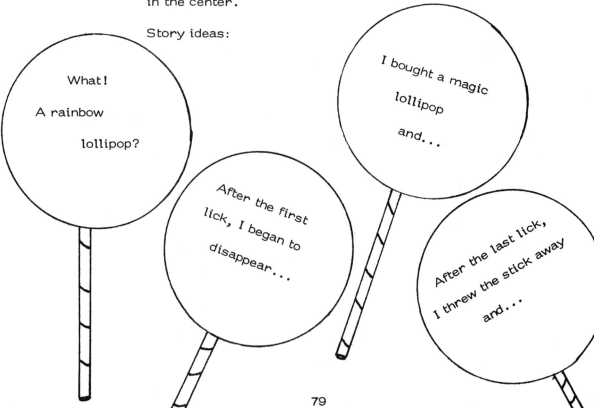

What!

A rainbow

lollipop?

I bought a magic

lollipop

and...

After the first
lick, I began to
disappear...

After the last lick,
I threw the stick away
and...

LOLLIPOP LAND

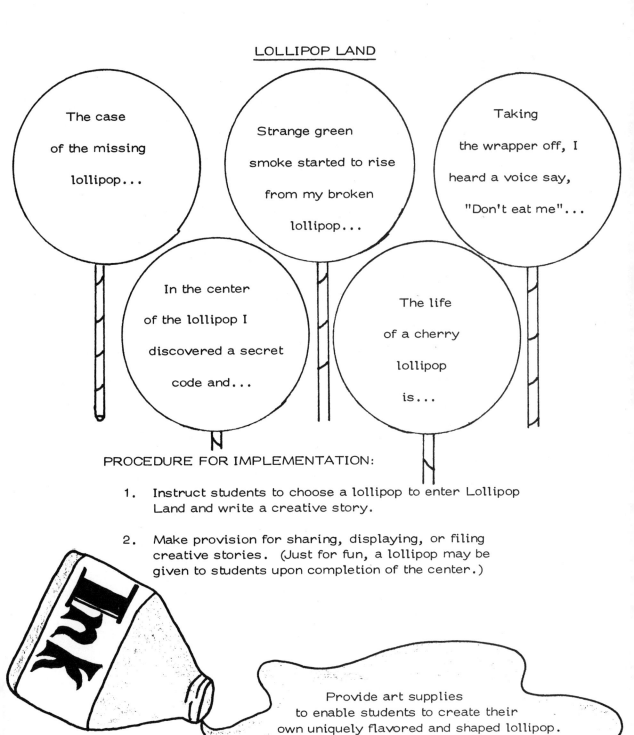

The case of the missing lollipop...

Strange green smoke started to rise from my broken lollipop...

Taking the wrapper off, I heard a voice say, "Don't eat me"...

In the center of the lollipop I discovered a secret code and...

The life of a cherry lollipop is...

PROCEDURE FOR IMPLEMENTATION:

1. Instruct students to choose a lollipop to enter Lollipop Land and write a creative story.

2. Make provision for sharing, displaying, or filing creative stories. (Just for fun, a lollipop may be given to students upon completion of the center.)

Ink

Provide art supplies to enable students to create their own uniquely flavored and shaped lollipop.

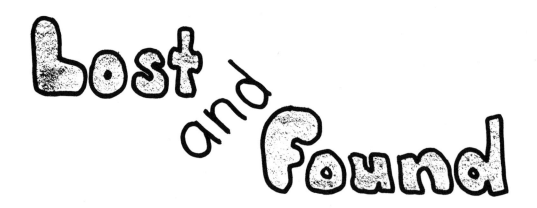

Lost and Found

PURPOSE:

After completing this center, the student should
be able to write an open-end story.

CENTER PREPARATION:

For the focal point of the center, make the following
advertisement:

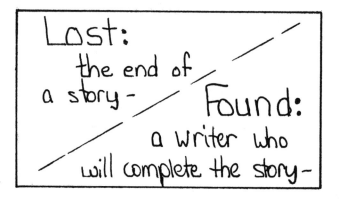

Cover the bulletin board with the classified section
of the newspaper. In the middle of the bulletin board
mount the advertisement.

LOST AND FOUND

PROCEDURE FOR IMPLEMENTATION:

1. Read an open-end story to introduce the center.
   Explain that an open-end story can be completed
   in different ways. Let the students decide possible
   outcomes for the story that has just been read.

2. Instruct students to write an open-end story and
   let someone in the group provide the story ending.

3. Make provision for sharing, displaying, or filing
   completed stories.

Provide time for the students
to dramatize the stories that have
been written.

The "Magic" Carpet

PURPOSE:

> After completing this center, the student should
> be able to express himself creatively through
> writing a story.

CENTER PREPARATION:

Arrange the center attractively. As a focal point
for the center make a Magic Carpet using eighteen
popsicle sticks, a piece of tagboard, and yarn
fringe. Print one Magic Carpet adventure on each
popsicle stick.

Adventure Ideas:

An elephant wants to take a ride...

A hungry tiger is sneaking up on you...
I have been caught in an avalanche...
My carpet is caught in a tall tree and torn...
Flying over the ocean, you spot some pirate ships...
A king orders me to give him my magic carpet...
My carpet is stolen while I'm sleeping...
I forgot the magic words to stop my carpet...
A fire-breathing dragon burns a hole in my carpet...
An elephant wants to take a ride...
As I was peering over the side of
    my carpet, I fell down, down...
Traveling over the mountains, the
    abominable snowman stopped me...

THE MAGIC CARPET

I took my teacher for a ride on my carpet...
An airplane is coming toward me. Watch out!...
While flying on the magic carpet, you come face
   to face with Skylab...
I begin my trip in the midst of an electrical storm...

PROCEDURE FOR IMPLEMENTATION:

1. Instruct students to pull out a fringe to find an
    idea to send them on an exciting adventure and
    write a creative story.

2. Provide time for students to write additional stories.

3. Make provision for sharing, displaying, or filing
    adventure stories.

Provide mural paper and art supplies
to enable students to illustrate their Magic
Carpet adventures.

Marooned Madness

PURPOSE:

> After completing this center, the student should
> be able to select an imaginary situation and write
> a creative story.

CENTER PREPARATION:

As a focal point for the center, make an outline of
an island including some physical features. Mount
the island picture on a bulletin board and arrange
the center attractively.

Make a diary from construction paper. On each page
of the diary print one of the following island adventures.

MAROONED MADNESS

The water supply is low...	I need to build shelter...	I think there might be someone else on this island...
I am hungry and...	I found footprints on the beach...	I woke up in the middle of the night and...
My radio is broken and I need to send a message...	My plans for escape are...	To keep from being lonesome I...

PROCEDURE FOR IMPLEMENTATION:

1. Instruct students to imagine they have been shipwrecked on an island. The students should consult the "Diary" ideas for motivation for an island adventure story.

2. Provide time for students to write additional stories.

3. Make provision for sharing, displaying, or filing adventure stories.

Provide art supplies for students to draw how they will look on the island. Pictures may be added to a mural on the island bulletin board.

Mushroom Maze

PURPOSE:

After completing this center, the student should be able to express appreciation for nature by writing a creative story.

CENTER PREPARATION:

Using tagboard and paints, make mushrooms. On each mushroom print one story idea. Place the mushrooms in the center.

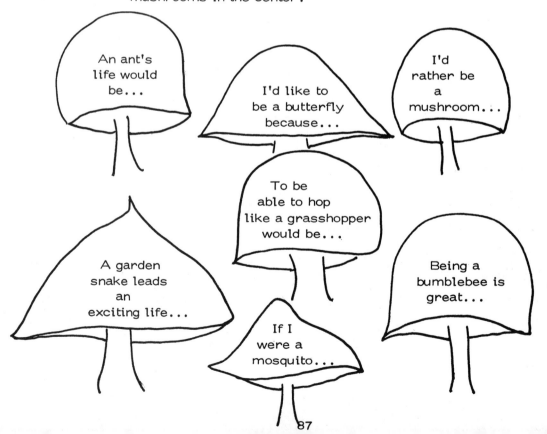

An ant's life would be...

I'd like to be a butterfly because...

I'd rather be a mushroom...

To be able to hop like a grasshopper would be...

A garden snake leads an exciting life...

If I were a mosquito...

Being a bumblebee is great...

MUSHROOM MAZE

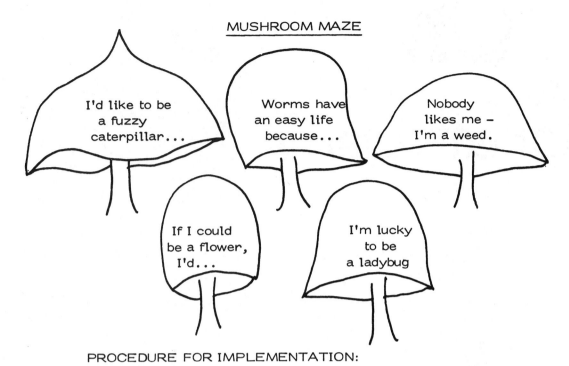

I'd like to be
a fuzzy
caterpillar...

Worms have
an easy life
because...

Nobody
likes me –
I'm a weed.

If I could
be a flower,
I'd...

I'm lucky
to be
a ladybug

PROCEDURE FOR IMPLEMENTATION:

1. To introduce the center, take a nature walk. Let
    the students discuss what they have seen.

2. Instruct students to select a mushroom idea and write
    a story.

3. Allow students to spend as much time in this center
    as they wish.

4. Make provision for sharing, displaying, or filing
    nature stories.

Make a nature bulletin board. Provide
art supplies for students to draw the living
thing they have written about. They may
make their own face on the living thing.

Oh Great Genie

PURPOSE:

After completing this center, the student should be able to express himself more creatively through writing and dramatics.

CENTER PREPARATION:

Arrange the center attractively using a Magic Pot as the focal point. The Magic Pot may be made from tagboard and spray painted gold.

OH GREAT GENIE

PROCEDURE FOR IMPLEMENTATION:

1. Tell students to rub the Magic Pot gently to summon a "genie" who can grant them one wish. Students are to write a story telling about their wish.

2. An activity sheet may be prepared for the students' stories.

3. Make provision for students to share completed stories in small groups.

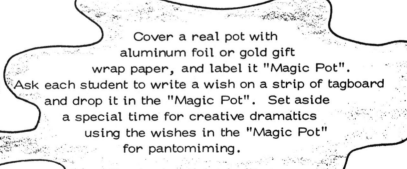

Cover a real pot with aluminum foil or gold gift wrap paper, and label it "Magic Pot". Ask each student to write a wish on a strip of tagboard and drop it in the "Magic Pot". Set aside a special time for creative dramatics using the wishes in the "Magic Pot" for pantomiming.

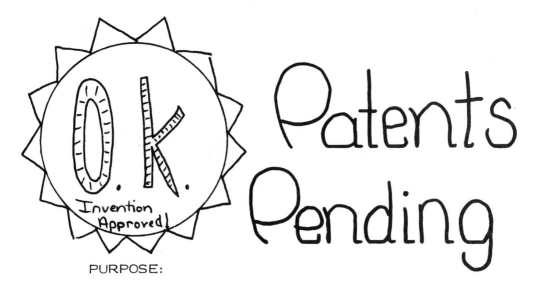

Patents Pending

PURPOSE:

> After completing this center, the student should be able to create a story about an imaginary invention.

CENTER PREPARATION:

Using tagboard and paints, make an imaginary invention and place on the bulletin board.

Print one story idea on a button or wheel. Attach the buttons and wheels to the imaginary invention.

Polluter-Diluter Machine

Super Scooper Machine

Hopper-Popper Machine

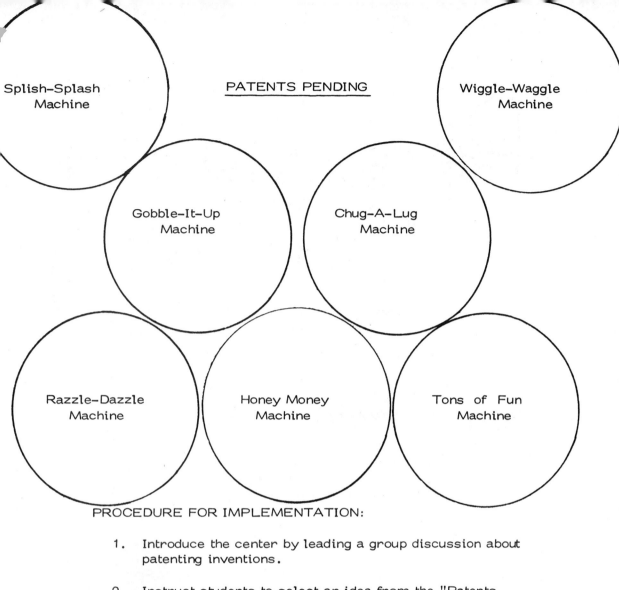

Splish–Splash Machine

PATENTS PENDING

Wiggle–Waggle Machine

Gobble–It–Up Machine

Chug–A–Lug Machine

Razzle–Dazzle Machine

Honey Money Machine

Tons of Fun Machine

PROCEDURE FOR IMPLEMENTATION:

1. Introduce the center by leading a group discussion about patenting inventions.

2. Instruct students to select an idea from the "Patents Pending" board and write a story about it.

3. Make provision for sharing, displaying, or filing invention stories.

Ink

Fill a box with the following items to be used by the students to create new inventions: styrofoam, toothpicks, string, glitter, wire, glue, pipe cleaners, washers, rubber bands, nuts and bolts, nails, foil, paper clips and brads.

Personality Reality

PURPOSE:

After completing this center, the student should be able to develop an awareness of personality characteristics and be able to write a paragraph describing his personality.

CENTER PREPARATION:

To make the center more interesting, make a large crystal ball and mount on the bulletin board.

Print the following caption:

Look in the Crystal Ball to Learn More About Yourself

PERSONALITY REALITY

PROCEDURE FOR IMPLEMENTATION:

1. Introduce the center by initiating a discussion of personality characteristics. Instruct students to write a descriptive paragraph about their personality. Paragraphs may be read aloud to allow the class to identify individual students through the personality descriptions.

2. Provide extra time for students to write a paragraph describing a friend's personality. Let students exchange paragraphs and try to identify the mystery personality.

3. Make provision for sharing, displaying, or filing personality paragraphs.

Prepare a "Mystery Personality"
bulletin board. Provide art supplies
for students to draw or paint their own portraits. After the portraits have been mounted,
members of the class will enjoy identifying
the mystery persons.

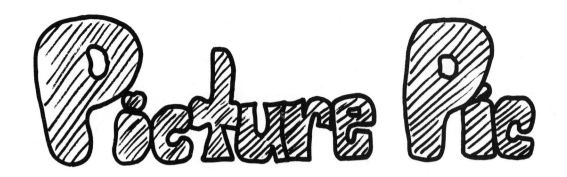

PURPOSE:

> After completing this center, the student should
> be able to use pictures to tell a story creatively.

CENTER PREPARATION:

Arrange the center by preparing the following
pictograms. Mount them in the center to motivate
students.

PICTURE PIC

PROCEDURE FOR IMPLEMENTATION:

1. Introduce the center by leading a class discussion concerning early means of communication. Explain that a pictogram is a symbol for a word:

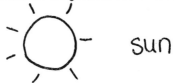 **sun**

   and an ideogram is a symbol for an idea.

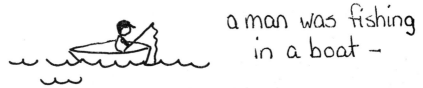 a man was fishing in a boat –

2. Instruct students to draw five pictograms and five ideograms.

3. Provide paper for students to send a message to a friend using pictograms and ideograms.

4. Encourage students to write stories using pictograms and ideograms.

5. Make provision for sharing, displaying, or filing completed activities.

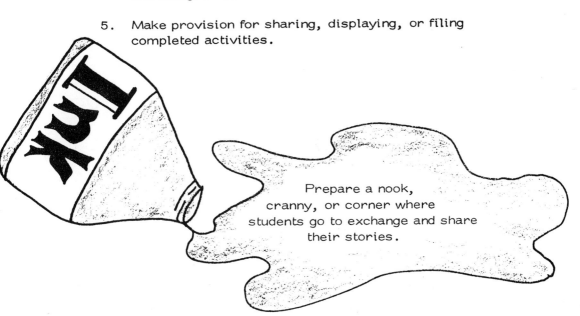

Prepare a nook, cranny, or corner where students go to exchange and share their stories.

PURPOSE:

> After completing this center, the student should be able to write a creative story, a poem, or a song.

CENTER PREPARATION:

Using tagboard and paints, make assorted flowers. On each flower print one story idea and arrange the flowers in the center.

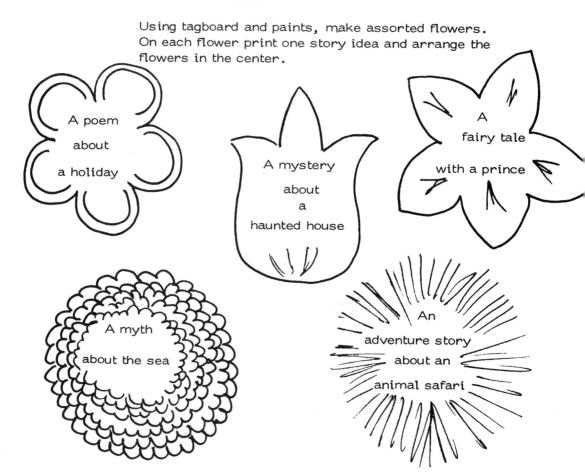

A poem about a holiday

A mystery about a haunted house

A fairy tale with a prince

A myth about the sea

An adventure story about an animal safari

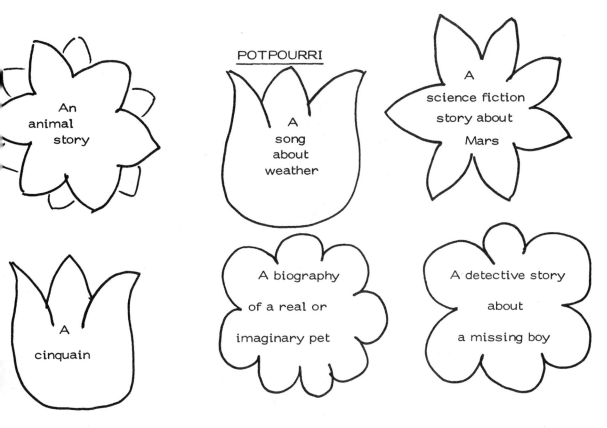

POTPOURRI

An animal story

A song about weather

A science fiction story about Mars

A cinquain

A biography of a real or imaginary pet

A detective story about a missing boy

PROCEDURE FOR IMPLEMENTATION:

1. Instruct students to select a flower idea and write a story, a poem, or a song.

2. Encourage students to write additional stories.

3. Make provision for sharing, displaying, or filing stories.

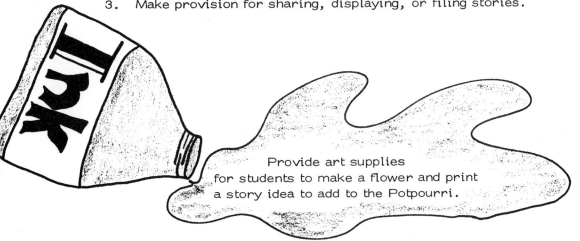

Provide art supplies for students to make a flower and print a story idea to add to the Potpourri.

Private Eye

PURPOSE:

> After completing this center, the student should
> be able to write a creative mystery story.

CENTER PREPARATION:

Arrange the center attractively. Using tagboard
and magic markers, make one large magnifying
glass. In the middle of the magnifying glass print
the following mysteries to be solved:

a.   Mrs. Brown's pie was stolen from her
     window and tracks were seen around the
     house.

b.   The puppy was missing from the dog house,
     and close by was found a pen with the initials
     G.R.T.

c.   Every night at 10:15 strange music is heard
     coming from the park.

d.   Children are reporting missing homework and
     bubble gum is left in its place.

e.   Hearing the knocking, Mother goes to the door
     and finds a secret message.

f.   The police get a telephone call from Mr. Green
     saying his refrigerator has been raided.

PRIVATE EYE

g. John goes to bed and under the pillow finds
   the message: Beware of B- - G- - - - -.

h. The Doughnut Shop was burglarized last night.
   The only clue found was a trail of cinnamon
   and sugar.

i. Each house on the block has a greasy doorknob.
   Who's got the greasy hands?

j. The message, "Doobells are coming," was
   found written on the school steps. A strange
   footprint was found nearby.

PROCEDURE FOR IMPLEMENTATION:

1. Introduce the center by reading a mystery story.

2. Instruct students to choose a mystery and solve it by
   writing a story.

3. Make provision for sharing, displaying, or filing
   mystery stories.

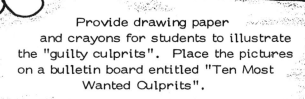

Provide drawing paper
and crayons for students to illustrate
the "guilty culprits". Place the pictures
on a bulletin board entitled "Ten Most
Wanted Culprits".

PURPOSE:

> After completing this activity, the student should
> be able to creatively substitute pictures for words.

CENTER PREPARATION:

Arrange the center including the Rebus story to
enable students to understand the concept of a rebus.

RE-BUS

PROCEDURE FOR IMPLEMENTATION:

1. Instruct students that a Rebus is a story consisting
    of pictures that suggest words or syllables. Students
    are to write a Rebus.

2. Make provision for sharing, displaying or filing
    stories. A bulletin board utilizing a large bus cut
    from colored paper as a background on which to
    pin stories would add interest.

Provide time for two
students to cooperate and write another
Re-

Rhythm and Rhyme

PURPOSE:

> After completing this center, the student should be able to write and illustrate a creative nursery rhyme.

CENTER PREPARATION:

To add interest to the center, enlarge on tagboard the "mod" Humpty Dumpty.

RHYTHM AND RHYME

PROCEDURE FOR IMPLEMENTATION:

1. To introduce the center, discuss the historical background of nursery rhymes. Let students share their favorite nursery rhymes.

2. Instruct students to select three of their favorite nursery rhymes and for each rhyme, create "mod" characters.

3. As a supplementary activity, students may enjoy creating a modern nursery rhyme. Provide paper and art supplies for students to write their nursery rhyme and illustrate it with "mod" characters.

4. Make provision for sharing, displaying, or filing nursery rhymes. (Students may wish to put their nursery rhymes together to make a booklet for the library table.)

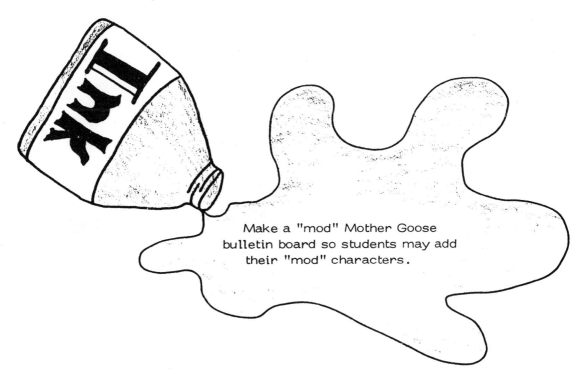

Make a "mod" Mother Goose bulletin board so students may add their "mod" characters.

Roving Reporters

PURPOSE:

> After completing this center, the student should
> be able to write a creative newspaper story.

CENTER PREPARATION:

Using drawing paper, make a large newspaper.
On each section, print one of the following headlines:

The Reporter	News	Sports
Space Men Encounter Strange Creature	Students Strike Predicted	Newly Created Sport Played Here

Sports	Editorials	Editorials
Eight-year-old boy Drafted by the Dolphins	Candy and ice cream should be eaten at any time. Higher Allowances for Cost of Living	New bedtimes... 11:30 p.m. Wanted – shorter school day

ROVING REPORTERS

Society Social event of the season... Wedding at Midnight	**T.V.** Don't miss the late late show. New program begins tonight.	**Women's Page** Cooking prize awarded for new recipe... Gabby's Gossip Corner
Comics New comic strips coming soon.	**Weather** Hat-snatching Wind is forecast. Sun not seen for Eleven Days	**Want Ads** Wanted: New Mother New Teacher School for Rent Sister for Sale

On a table in the creative writing center, place the large newspaper.

PROCEDURE FOR IMPLEMENTATION:

1. In small groups, introduce the center by reading the newspaper. Discuss the different newspaper sections.

2. Instruct students to read the large newspaper in the center, select a title, and write a creative newspaper article.

3. Give each student a newspaper assignment related to classroom news and events.

4. Compile the student articles and make a class newspaper.

5. Make provision for sharing, displaying, or filing newspaper articles.

Provide paper and art supplies for students to use in preparing newspaper advertisements. Add the advertisements to the class newspaper.

PURPOSE:

> After completing this center, the student should
> be able to make comparisons between two seasons
> and express them creatively.

CENTER PREPARATION:

Arrange the center attractively. Using tagboard
and tempera paint make autumn leaves and a pumpkin,
snowflakes and a snowman, wind and a kite, and
a sprinkling can and flowers. Mount the pictures on
a bulletin board in the center.

SEASON SNAPSHOT

Print the directions on a piece of tagboard and place in the center.

> Choose two seasons and compare their similarities and differences. Include these ideas in your comparisons:
>
> | | | |
> |---|---|---|
> | sports | holidays | weather |
> | foods | customs | nature |
> | clothing | chores | entertainment |
>
> Write a creative story comparing two seasons.

PROCEDURE FOR IMPLEMENTATION:

1. Instruct the students to follow the directions in the center to complete the activity.

2. Make provision for sharing, displaying, or filing season snapshots.

Winter

Spring

Provide magazines, scissors, paste, and paper for students to make a collage comparing two seasons.

Shooting Match

PURPOSE:

After completing this center, the student should be able to work in a small group setting to create a story.

CENTER PREPARATION:

Enlarge and paint the Shooting Match cowboy on tagboard to be used as the focal point for the center. Print one word on each tagboard strip.

Word cards:

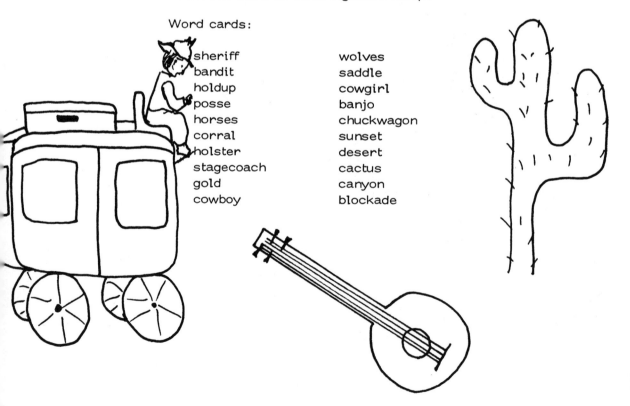

sheriff	wolves
bandit	saddle
holdup	cowgirl
posse	banjo
horses	chuckwagon
corral	sunset
holster	desert
stagecoach	cactus
gold	canyon
cowboy	blockade

SHOOTING MATCH

PROCEDURE FOR IMPLEMENTATION:

1. Instruct students to follow the game directions.

    > 1. The cards are shuffled and placed in the center of the group.
    >
    > 2. The first player draws a card and must include the word on the card in the sentence he provides for the story.
    >
    > 3. One member of the group will act as the secretary and record each sentence.
    >
    > 4. The next player draws a card, makes a sentence using the word, and adds it to the story.
    >
    > 5. Players continue to draw cards and add to the story until all the word cards have been used.
    >
    > 6. The story should be checked to make sure it is in logical order.

2. Make provision for sharing, displaying, or filing the Shooting Match story.

Provide mural paper to be used for story illustrations. Encourage each member of the group to add to the mural.

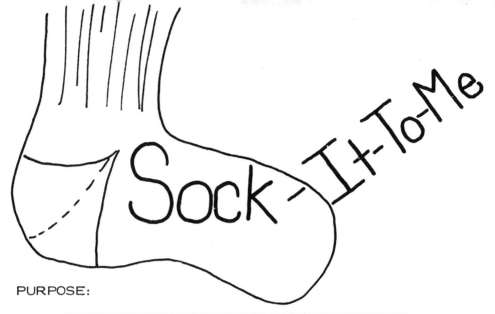

Sock-It-To-Me

PURPOSE:

After completing this center, the student should
be able to create puppet characters and develop
and write a puppet play.

CENTER PREPARATION:

Arrange a creative puppet corner. Provide the
following materials:

socks	buttons	sequins
needles	yarn	stuffing (cloth
thread	felt	or paper)

As an example, prepare a puppet and place in the
center. Using a large cardboard box, make a puppet
stage.

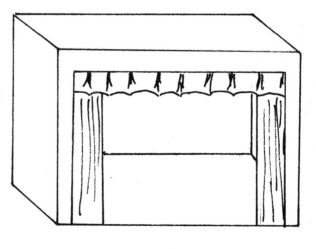

SOCK–IT–TO–ME

Prepare the following list of puppet characters:

clown	elephant	postman	scientist
dog	old lady	cat	teacher
frog	doctor	little girl	cowboy
nurse	elf	little boy	astronaut
lion	farmer	mouse	horse

PROCEDURE FOR IMPLEMENTATION:

1. Instruct students to choose two characters and make two sock puppets.

2. After puppets have been completed, direct students to write a play involving the two puppet characters.

3. Provide time for students to present their puppet play.

Provide art supplies so students may draw background scenery for their puppet play.

Spaced Out

PURPOSE:

> After completing this center, the student should be able to express himself more creatively.

CENTER PREPARATION:

Arrange a large bulletin board to serve as the background for this center. Make a spaceship from tagboard to place on the bulletin board. Cut stars and paint them yellow or cover them with foil. Print one Spaced Out story title on each star and mount the stars.

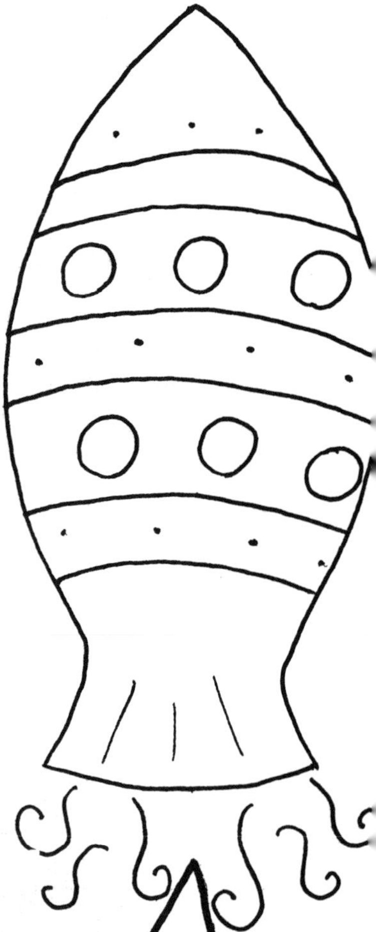

Planet Collision

Trip Through the Milky Way

The Tiny Speck

The Stalled Space Ship

The Falling Star

A New Discovery

The Bright Light

SPACED OUT

PROCEDURE FOR IMPLEMENTATION:

1. Instruct students to select a story title and write a story.

2. Allow each student to spend as much time in this center as he wishes. Some students might elect to write several stories to be made into a book complete with illustrations.

3. Make provision for sharing, displaying, or filing Spaced Out stories.

Designate a nook, crannie or corner and plan a time for students to dramatize stories.

Spellbound

PURPOSE:

> After completing this center, the student should be able to "break a spell" and express himself creatively.

CENTER PREPARATION:

Arrange the center attractively. On a bulletin board place a picture of a witch stirring her pot of "spells".

On strips of tagboard, print the following spellbound ideas:

Save me, I'm a toad...
Once a prince, now a horse...
When I opened my mouth, I started barking...
Now I'm a buzzing bee...
Help, I'm stuck in a teapot...
I've been turned into a two-neaded monster...

SPELLBOUND

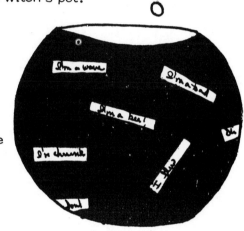

I've shrunk, look at me...
The spell turned me into a grouch...
Now I'm a wave in the ocean...
All I did was trick the witch...
I felt funny when I started flying...
I looked in the mirror and I had a fluffy tail...
I woke up and I was a flea on my dog...
Let me out of this goldfish bowl...
Suddenly I am a head of cauliflower...

Mount the spellbound ideas on the witch's pot.

PROCEDURE FOR IMPLEMENTATION:

1. Instruct students to select an idea and to use the "break the spell" by writing a creative story.

2. Provide time for students to write additional stories.

3. Make provision for sharing, displaying, or filing spellbound stories.

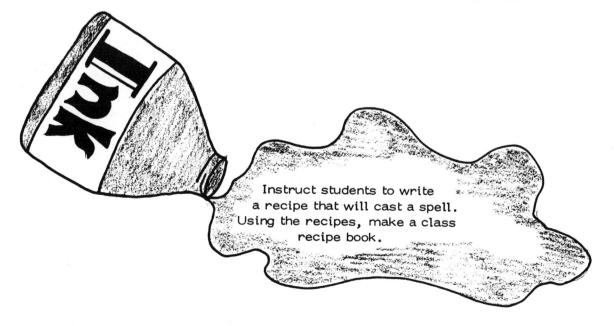

Instruct students to write a recipe that will cast a spell. Using the recipes, make a class recipe book.

Stan the Man

PURPOSE:

> After completing this center, the student should be able to write a story expressing himself creatively.

CENTER PREPARATION:

To motivate the students, print the story starter ideas on a large piece of tagboard and arrange attractively in the center.

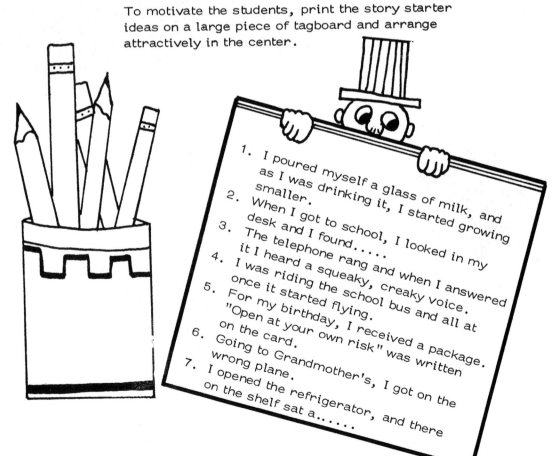

1. I poured myself a glass of milk, and as I was drinking it, I started growing smaller.
2. When I got to school, I looked in my desk and I found.....
3. The telephone rang and when I answered it I heard a squeaky, creaky voice.
4. I was riding the school bus and all at once it started flying.
5. For my birthday, I received a package. "Open at your own risk" was written on the card.
6. Going to Grandmother's, I got on the wrong plane.
7. I opened the refrigerator, and there on the shelf sat a......

STAN THE MAN

PROCEDURE FOR IMPLEMENTATION:

1. Instruct the students to select a story starter idea and complete the story.

2. Provide time for students to write additional stories.

3. Make provision for the student to share his story if he wishes.

Provide a time for the students to present a puppet show. With finger puppets have the stories dramatized.

PURPOSE:

After completing this center, the student should
be able to write a creative story.

CENTER PREPARATION:

Using tagboard and tempera paint, enlarge the
shopping center and place in the creative writing
center. Print the following title on the front of
each store:

grocery store   restaurant
drug store   sporting goods store
toy shop   dress shop
pet shop   candy store
gift shop   jewelry store
beauty salon   bakery

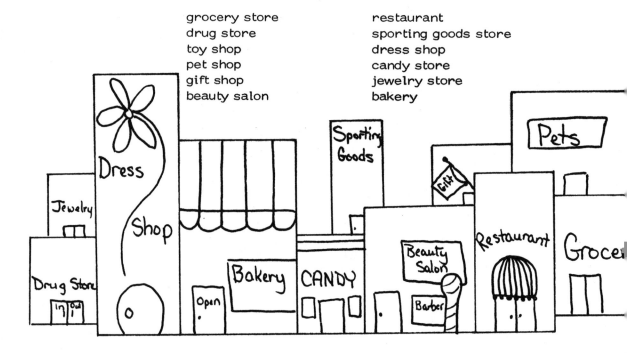

STORES GALORE

On a chart, print the following directions:

> 1. Select a store in the shopping center and give it a name.
>
> 2. Write a story and include the following ideas:
>
>   What will you sell?
>   What are the prices?
>   Who will you employ?
>   How will you arrange the store?
>   How will you advertise your business?
>   What will make your business a success?

PROCEDURE FOR IMPLEMENTATION:

1. Introduce the center by leading a group discussion of businesses and the services they provide for a city.

2. Instruct students to read and follow the center directions to write a story about a store of the future.

3. Make provision for sharing, displaying, or filing completed stories.

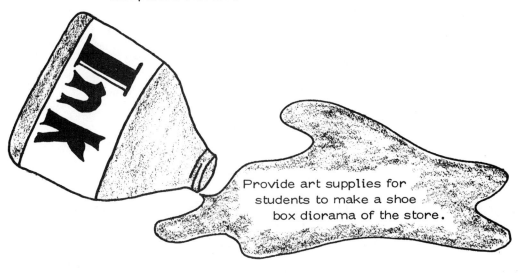

Provide art supplies for students to make a shoe box diorama of the store.

Surprise Box

PURPOSE:

After completing this center, the student should
be able to write a creative story using different
objects.

CENTER PREPARATION:

Arrange the center attractively. As a center of
interest, paint a square cardboard box to resemble
a jack-in-the-box. Fill the box with a variety of
objects. Some suggested objects are:

bean	onion	flashlight
piece of puzzle	glove	bobby pin
handkerchief	bow	plastic flower
paper cup	popsicle stick	measuring spoons
key	fork	penny
ball	comb	marble
string	rubber band	bottle cap
clock	toy car	ring
magic marker	bracelet	paper clip
doll	pencil	ribbon

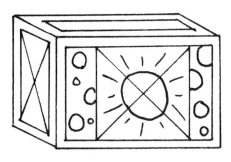

SURPRISE BOX

Print the following directions on a large chart:

> Draw three objects from the "Surprise Box".
>
> Using these objects as main characters,
> write a story about their adventure.

PROCEDURE FOR IMPLEMENTATION:

1. Instruct students to follow the directions on the large
   chart in the center and write a creative story.

2. Make provision for sharing, displaying or filing
   the surprise stories.

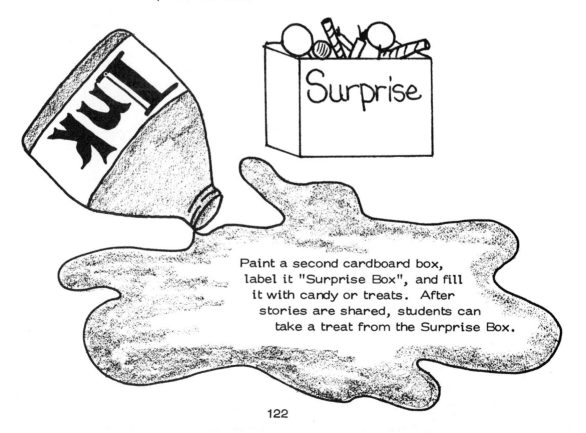

Paint a second cardboard box,
label it "Surprise Box", and fill
it with candy or treats. After
stories are shared, students can
take a treat from the Surprise Box.

Suspense Theater

PURPOSE:

> After completing this center, the student should
> be able to dramatize a story title and express
> himself creatively.

CENTER PREPARATION:

Arrange the center attractively. On the bulletin
board make a theater marquee. On the marquee
print "Now Playing, SUSPENSE THEATER, Featuring
___?___ (Class) ___."

Cover a shoe box with contact paper. On the lid print
"Coming Soon". Inside the box place strips of tagboard
with the following movie titles:

The Apple Tree Mystery	The Two-faced Monster
The Case of the Missing Shoe	The Claw that Scratched

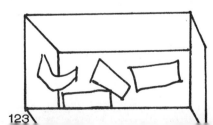

SUSPENSE THEATER

Mystery of the Purple Lady
The Missing Treasure Chest
Creature from Outer Space
The Robbery of the Lemonade
  Stand
The Giant Octopus
The Case of the Holeless
  Doughnut
The Lost Halo
The Cowboy Rides Again

Lost in a Cave
The Robot Invasion
Captain Blood and
  Mr. Bones
The Missing Doornob
The Pirates Strike Again
Mystery of the Missing
  Pencil
Mysterious Fruitcake
Green Giant Meets Superboy

PROCEDURE FOR IMPLEMENTATION:

1. Introduce the center by initiating a discussion of the game "Charades". Instruct students to work in small groups to select a movie title and dramatize it without speaking. Allow the other students three minutes to guess the movie title being dramatized.

2. Encourage students to select one of the movie titles to be used to write a creative story.

3. Make provision for sharing, displaying, or filing movie stories.

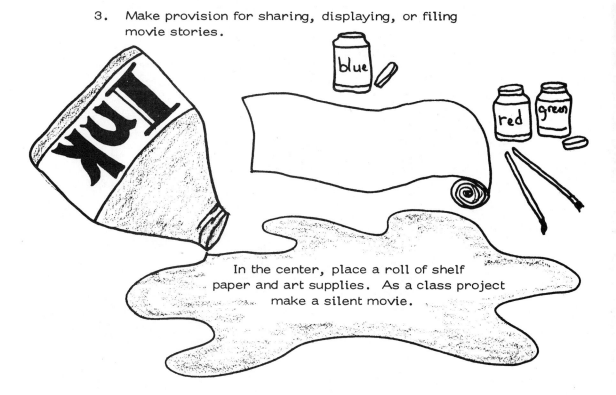

In the center, place a roll of shelf paper and art supplies. As a class project make a silent movie.

Talking Toys

PURPOSE:

After completing this center, the student should be able to write a story expressing the imaginary feelings of an inanimate object.

CENTER PREPARATION:

Ask each student to bring a toy from home. Place the toys in a decorated cardboard box. Using the toy box as a focal point, arrange the center in a quiet corner of the room.

TALKING TOYS

On a chart, print the following directions:

Look in the "toy box" and think of a toy you would like to be. Imagine that you have just come off the assembly line in a toy factory. Write a story and include some of these ideas.

1. What kind of a toy are you?
2. How and from what were you made?
3. Where will you be shipped?
4. How will you travel?
5. Who will be your friends in the store where you will be sold?
6. How much will you cost?
7. Who will buy you?
8. Tell about the rest of your life.

PROCEDURE FOR IMPLEMENTATION:

1. Instruct students to look in the toy box and find an idea that will begin their life as a toy.

2. Students may then follow the center directions and write a story.

3. Encourage students to write additional stories.

4. Make provision for sharing, displaying, or filing stories.

Provide art supplies for the students to use to illustrate their stories. On a bulletin board, display the pictures.

Tell It Like It Is

PURPOSE:

> After completing this center, the student should
> be able to creatively write descriptive phrases
> and paragraphs.

CENTER PREPARATION:

As a focal point for the center paint or cover a
cardboard box. Fill the box with items that can
be easily described. Some suggested items are:

stuffed animal	string of beads
toy car	ball
soap	feather
brush	block
nail	sponge
doll	bell
scarf	glove

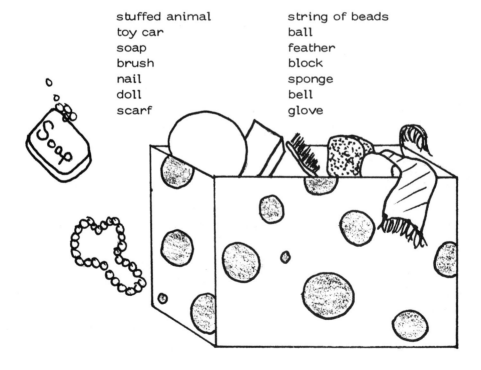

TELL IT LIKE IT IS

PROCEDURE FOR IMPLEMENTATION:

1. To introduce the center, give each student an apple. After examining and eating the apple, let students make a list of words that describe the apple. Discuss and discover words that best describe the apple.

2. Instruct students to select four objects from the box and describe them by using words and phrases.

3. Provide additional time for students to write a descriptive paragraph about an object found outside.

4. Make provision for sharing, displaying or filing descriptive phrases and paragraphs.

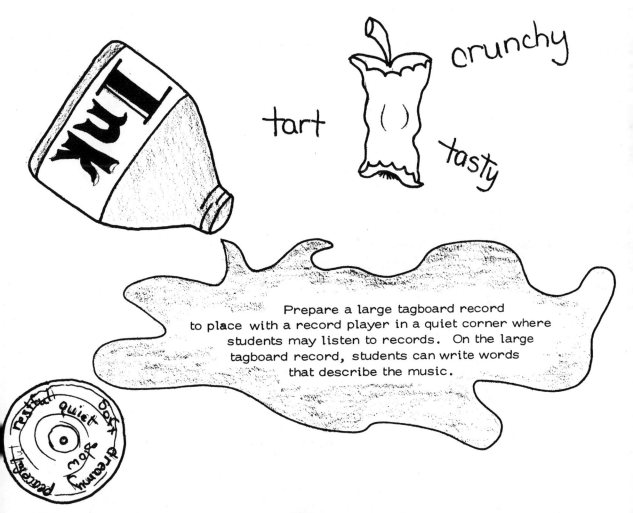

tart

crunchy

tasty

Prepare a large tagboard record to place with a record player in a quiet corner where students may listen to records. On the large tagboard record, students can write words that describe the music.

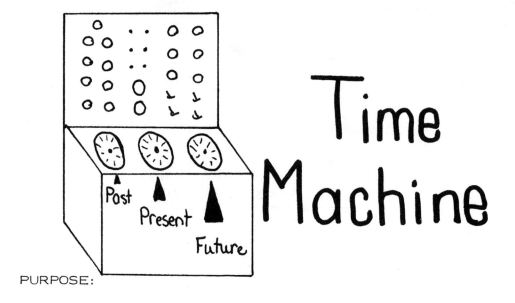

Time Machine

PURPOSE:

> After completing this center, the student should be able to express changes influenced by time.

CENTER PREPARATION:

Arrange the center attractively. As a focal point for the center, make a Time Machine. On three cardboard circles, print events that occurred in the past, present, and future. Attach the cardboard circles to the Time Machine with brass fasteners.

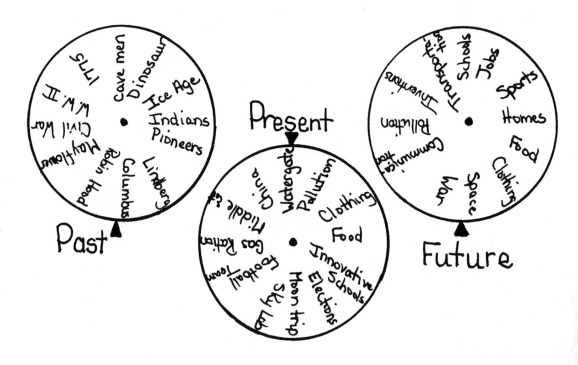

TIME MACHINE

PROCEDURE FOR IMPLEMENTATION:

1. Prepare directions that instruct students to select a time period by turning one cardboard circle. Students are to write about their visit in the Time Machine.

2. Make provision for sharing, displaying, or filing Time Machine stories.

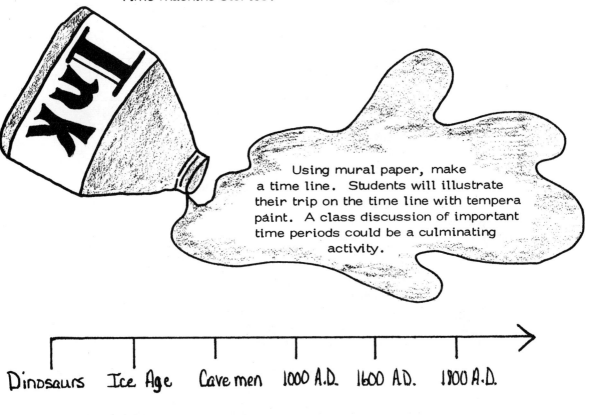

Using mural paper, make a time line. Students will illustrate their trip on the time line with tempera paint. A class discussion of important time periods could be a culminating activity.

Dinosaurs   Ice Age   Cave men   1000 A.D.   1600 A.D.   1800 A.D.

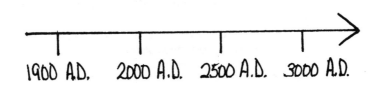

1900 A.D.   2000 A.D.   2500 A.D.   3000 A.D.

Trash Can

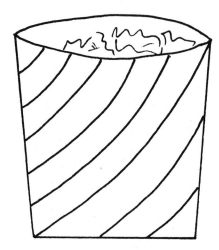

PURPOSE:

> After completing this center, the student should be able to write a creative solution to a pollution problem.

CENTER PREPARATION:

In the creative writing center, place an attractively decorated trash can. Fill the trash can with the following items:

tin can	gum wrapper
milk carton	paper bag
pop bottle	paper plate
plastic bag	cigarette
paper napkin	Kleenex
plastic fork	plastic bottle
bread wrapper	egg carton
bottle cap	shoe box

On a chart print the following directions and place in the center.

> 1. Look in the trash can and select an object that contributes to our pollution problem.
>
> 2. Write a story telling how to eliminate the pollution caused by this object.

TRASH CAN

PROCEDURE FOR IMPLEMENTATION:

1. Introduce the center by leading a group discussion concerning pollution. Encourage students to suggest ways of overcoming pollution problems.

2. Instruct students to read the chart, follow the directions, and write a creative story.

3. Provide additional time for students to write a story about a pollution problem that might occur in the year 2000.

4. Make provision for sharing, displaying, or filing the creative stories.

Take the students on a field trip around the school building and grounds to observe the pollution problems. Write a short paragraph telling how to reduce the problems.

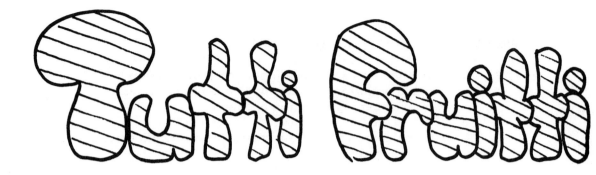

PURPOSE:

> After completing this center, the student should
> be able to write a creative poem.

CENTER PREPARATION:

Arrange the center attractively. As a focal point,
make a "Tutti Fruitti" tree filled with goodies.

TUTTI FRUITTI

On each "goody" print a word to be used as a poem idea.

rain	flowers	cowboy	holiday
sunshine	trees	wind	storm
candy	animal	snow	cloud
school	car	fairy	water
happiness	cake	sadness	food

PROCEDURE FOR IMPLEMENTATION:

1. Introduce the center by leading a discussion concerning different types of poetry.

2. Divide the students into small groups and instruct them to select a "goody" to use to write a poem.

3. Provide materials for illustrating the poems.

4. Allow students to spend as much time in this center as they wish.

5. Compile the poems into a class poetry book.

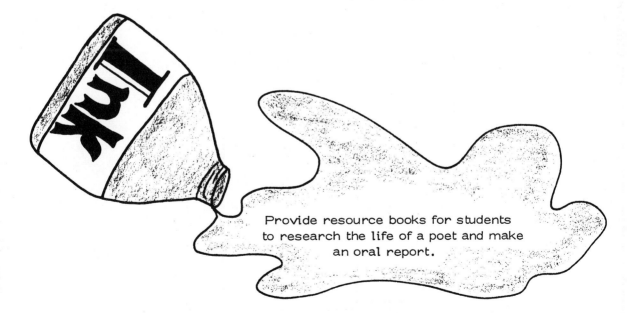

Provide resource books for students to research the life of a poet and make an oral report.

V.IP'S

PURPOSE:

After completing this center, the student should be able to write a creative autobiography.

CENTER PREPARATION:

Secure a cardboard refrigerator box and place it in a nook, cranny or corner. Make a door in the box large enough for a student to enter, and place a chair inside the box.

V.I.P.'S

PROCEDURE FOR IMPLEMENTATION:

1. Introduce the center by leading a group discussion about autobiographies.

2. Instruct students to write an autobiography, including elements from their past, present, and future life.

3. The writing can be done in the V.I.P. room.

4. Make provision for sharing, displaying, or filing autobiographies.

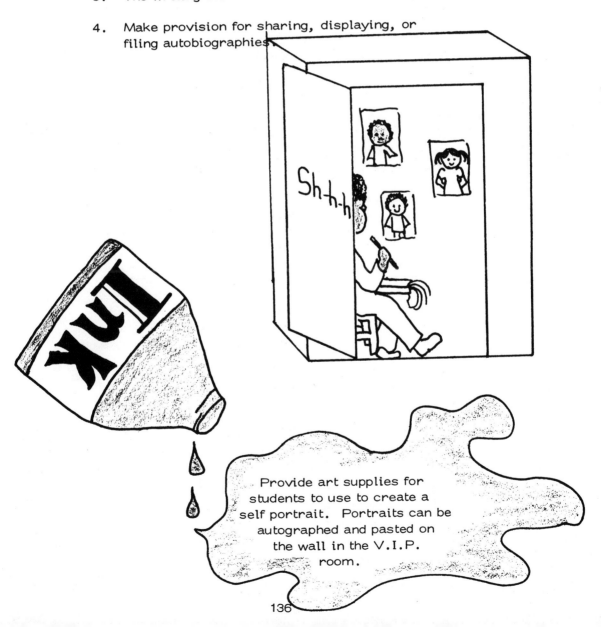

Provide art supplies for students to use to create a self portrait. Portraits can be autographed and pasted on the wall in the V.I.P. room.

PURPOSE:

> After completing this center, the student should
> be able to write a paragraph describing a specific
> occupation.

CENTER PREPARATION:

Select a quiet corner and hang a clothesline. Print
the following occupations on index cards:

dog catcher	policeman	astronaut
popsicle man	teacher	secretary
telephone lineman	dairy farmer	bricklayer
garbage man	housewife	miner
bartender	tailor	nurse
brush salesman	popcorn vender	plumber
pilot	cook	gardener
taxi driver	train conductor	musician
beautician	mortician	milkman
taxidermist	mechanic	chimney sweep

Using clothespins, fasten eight occupation cards to the
clothesline. Idea cards can be changed daily.

WHAT'S YOUR LINE

PROCEDURE FOR IMPLEMENTATION:

1. Introduce the center by leading a group discussion about community helpers and their role in society.

2. Instruct students to select a card from the clothesline and write a paragraph that creatively describes the occupation.

3. Provide time for students to write additional paragraphs.

4. Place the paragraphs in a covered shoe box.

5. As a group activity, students can take a paragraph out of the box and try to identify the occupation.

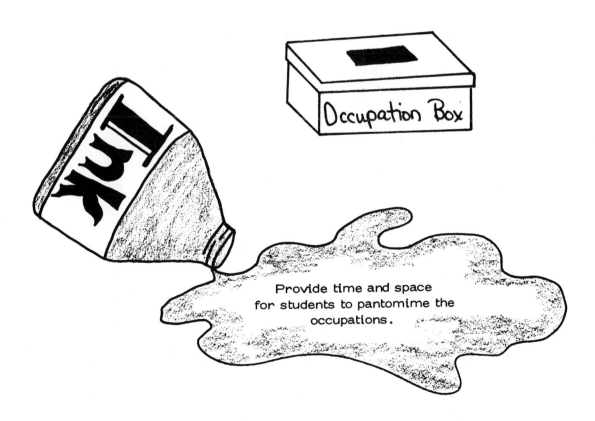

Provide time and space for students to pantomime the occupations.

YO-HO-HO

PURPOSE:

> After completing this center, the student should
> be able to write a creative adventure story.

CENTER PREPARATION:

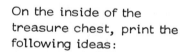

As a focal point for the center, make a large
treasure chest.

On the inside of the
treasure chest, print the
following ideas:

1. A pirate ship is approaching...
2. The other half of the map is missing...
3. While digging for gold, I...
4. My parrot gave the secret away...
5. Pegleg Pirate is after me...
6. Surprise attack at Pirate's Cove...
7. In the treasure chest I found...
8. All ashore, It's every man for himself...
9. Quick! Hoist the flag...
10. Move in closer, we'll board the ship...

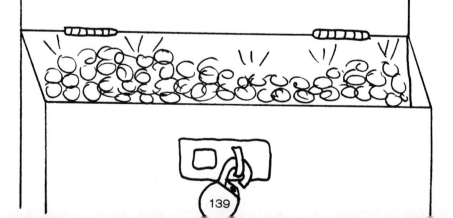

YO-HO-HO

PROCEDURE FOR IMPLEMENTATION:

1. To stimulate interest read a pirate story. Lead a discussion of "pirate days".

2. Instruct students to open the treasure chest and select an adventure idea to use in writing a story.

3. Encourage students to write additional stories. Some might enjoy writing stories explaining the disappearance of pirates.

4. Make provision for sharing, displaying, or filing the completed stories.

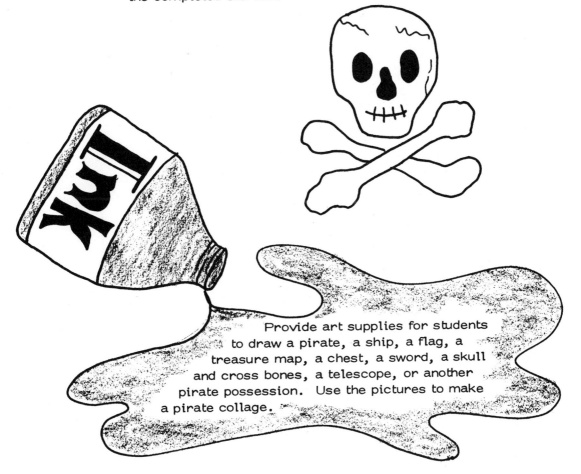

Provide art supplies for students to draw a pirate, a ship, a flag, a treasure map, a chest, a sword, a skull and cross bones, a telescope, or another pirate possession. Use the pictures to make a pirate collage.

Notes

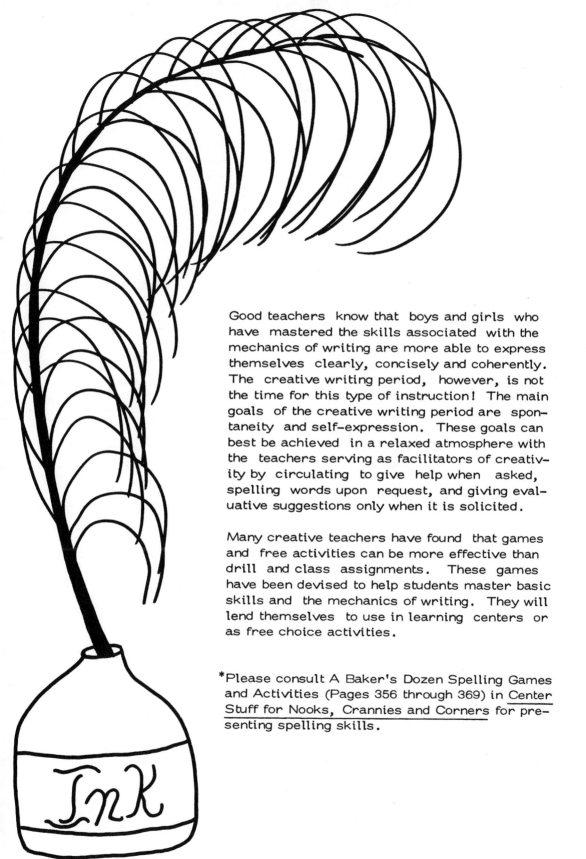

Good teachers know that boys and girls who have mastered the skills associated with the mechanics of writing are more able to express themselves clearly, concisely and coherently. The creative writing period, however, is not the time for this type of instruction! The main goals of the creative writing period are spontaneity and self-expression. These goals can best be achieved in a relaxed atmosphere with the teachers serving as facilitators of creativity by circulating to give help when asked, spelling words upon request, and giving evaluative suggestions only when it is solicited.

Many creative teachers have found that games and free activities can be more effective than drill and class assignments. These games have been devised to help students master basic skills and the mechanics of writing. They will lend themselves to use in learning centers or as free choice activities.

*Please consult A Baker's Dozen Spelling Games and Activities (Pages 356 through 369) in Center Stuff for Nooks, Crannies and Corners for presenting spelling skills.

BEAT THE CLOCK

PURPOSE:

> After completing this activity, the student should be able to understand the logical sequence in a paragraph.

Preparation Directions:

1. Select eight paragraphs.

2. Write each sentence of the paragraph on a separate strip of tagboard.

3. Place each paragraph in an envelope.

4. Provide an egg timer or kitchen timer.

5. One or two players may play this game.

Player Directions:

1. Each player chooses an envelope containing one paragraph.

2. The timer is set!

3. Players attempt to put the sentence strips in sequence to form a paragraph.

4. The player who completes a paragraph before the timer rings wins.

THE BIG "C"

PURPOSE:

> After completing this activity, the student should be able to use capital letters correctly.

Preparation Directions:

1. Enlarge the playing board below on tagboard to be used as a game board.

2. Provide markers for each player.

3. Write words and sentences on small tagboard cards, omitting capital letters.

4. Two or three players may play this game.

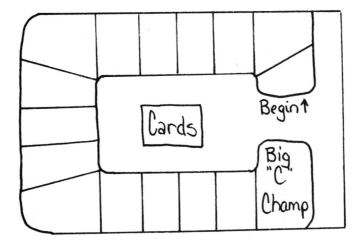

Player Directions:

1. Each player chooses a marker and places it on the board.

2. One player draws a card and reads the word or sentence aloud.

3. He then tells the word or words that need to be capitalized.

4. If he is able to make the correct changes, he moves ahead one space. If he cannot make the changes, he moves back one space.

5. The first player to reach the Finish wins the game.

COMMA CONFUSION

PURPOSE:

> After completing this activity, the student should
> be able to use commas correctly.

Preparation Directions:

1. Enlarge the playing board below on tagboard to be used
   as a game board.

2. Provide markers for each player.

3. Using a small cube of wood, make a die.

4. On ten strips of tagboard write sentences that contain
   commas. On ten other strips of tagboard, write sentences
   with the commas misplaced.

5. Two or four players may play this game.

Player Directions:

1. The sentence cards are placed face down in the middle
   of the board and each player chooses a marker.

2. The first player rolls the die and moves the correct number
   of spaces. He draws a card and tells if the commas are
   correct in the sentence. If the sentence is incorrect, he
   must tell where the commas should be placed.

3. When a player cannot give a correct answer, he moves
   back one space.

4. The game continues until one player reaches the Winner's
   Box.

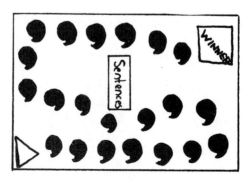

CRAZY CARDS

PURPOSE:

> After completing this activity, the student should be able to use the dictionary to improve alphabetizing skills.

Preparation Directions:

1. On forty index cards print nouns, each beginning with a different letter.

2. On six cards print "crazy card".

3. Two or three players may play this game.

Player Directions:

1. Shuffle the cards and deal five cards to each player. Place the remaining cards in the middle.

2. The player holding a card with a word beginning with "A" places the card in the middle. If no player holds a card with a word beginning with "A", the player who holds a card with a word that is closest to "A" can start the game.

3. Players continue to place words on cards in the middle in alphabetical order. If a player cannot follow alphabetical order, he draws cards from the stack until he can play.

4. If a player draws a "crazy card", the player can start the game over with any letter in the alphabet.

5. The first player to run out of cards wins.

146

DRIBBLE AND DESCRIBE

PURPOSE:

> After completing the activity, the student should
> be able to use descriptive words.

Preparation Directions:

1. Enlarge the playing board below on tagboard to be used
   as a game board.

2. Provide markers for each player.

3. On twenty strips of tagboard, write simple
   sentences.

4. Two or three players may play
   this game.

Player Directions:

1. Each player chooses a marker and places it on the board.

2. The cards are shuffled and placed face down.

3. The first player draws a card. He reads the sentence
   aloud and adds a word or words describing the noun
   in the sentence.

4. For each descriptive word he uses, he can take one dribble.

5. Players continue to take turns, moving up and down the
   board until one player has twenty points. Each basket
   scores two points.

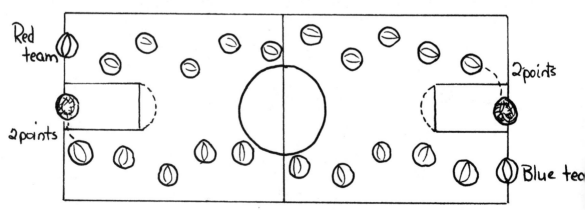

147

EASY AS PIE

PURPOSE:

> After completing this activity, the student should be able to make comparisons using descriptive words.

Preparation Directions:

1. Enlarge the playing board below on tagboard to be used as a game board.

2. Provide markers for each player.

3. Using a tagboard circle and a brass paper fastener, make a spinner.

4. Two players may play this game.

Player Directions:

1. Choose a marker and place it on the board.

2. The first player flips the spinner and moves the correct number of spaces. He must complete the comparison on the space.  -... as red as an apple....

3. When the player cannot give a comparison, he moves back one space.

4. The first player to reach the Finish wins.

GRAB BAG

PURPOSE:

> After completing this center, the student should be able to determine when to use the correct punctuation mark.

Preparation Directions:

1. Using felt or other materials, make a drawstring bag.

2. On thirty-five strips of tagboard, write sentences omitting the correct punctuation.

3. Four players may play this game.

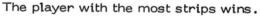

Player Directions:

1. The sentence strips are placed in the bag.

2. The first player draws a strip and corrects the punctuation. If he answers correctly, he can keep the strip. If his answer is incorrect, he must put the strip back into the bag.

3. The game continues until all the strips have been corrected.

4. The player with the most strips wins.

HOPSCOTCH

PURPOSE:

> After completing this activity, the student should be able to recognize and use a comma, an exclamation mark, a period, a question mark, and quotation marks.

Preparation Directions:

1. Use chalk or masking tape to outline a hopscotch diagram.

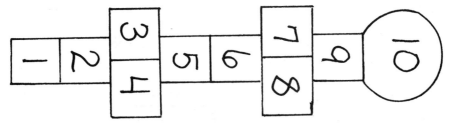

2. On index cards print the following punctuation marks: comma, exclamation mark, period, question mark, and quotation marks.

3. Provide two bean bags.

4. Two players may play this game.

Player Directions:

1. The punctuation cards are placed face down and each player chooses a bean bag.

2. The first player throws his bean bag on No. 1 and draws a card. He must give a sentence that requires the punctuation mark on the card.

3. If the player uses the correct punctuation mark, he gets another turn. If he is incorrect, the other player takes a turn.

4. Players must move from spaces 1 to 10, turn around and move back to 1; the first player to reach 1 the second time wins.

PERIOD PUZZLERS

PURPOSE:

> After completing this activity, the student should be able to identify complete sentences.

Preparation Directions:

1. Mount two magazine pictures on separate sheets of tagboard 9" x 12".

2. Cut each tagboard picture into ten puzzle pieces, and place in separate boxes.

3. On the back of each puzzle piece write either a phrase or a complete sentence.

4. Two players may play the game.

Player Directions:

1. Each player selects a puzzle box and scrambles the pieces.

2. The first player draws a puzzle piece and reads the group of words. He must tell if it is a phrase or a complete sentence.

3. If he answers correctly he may keep the puzzle piece. If his answer is incorrect, he returns the puzzle piece to the box.

4. The next player takes his turn.

5. The first player to complete his puzzle wins.

PUNCTUATION PARADISE

PURPOSE:

> After completing this activity, the student should
> be able to use punctuation marks correctly.

Preparation Directions:

1. Enlarge the playing board below on tagboard to be
   used as a game board.

2. Provide markers for each player.

3. Using a small cube of wood, make a die.

4. Two or three players may play this game.

Player Directions:

1. Each player chooses a marker and places it on the board.

2. The first player rolls the die and moves the correct
   number of spaces. He must give a sentence that contains
   the punctuation mark on the space.

3. When a player cannot give a correct sentence, he moves
   back two spaces.

4. The game continues until a player reaches "Paradise".

QUOTATION QUANDARY

PURPOSE:

> After completing this activity, the student should
> be able to use quotation marks correctly.

Preparation Directions:

1. On strips of tagboard, write twenty-four sentences
   needing quotation marks that have been omitted.

Hi Betsy, said Sue.

2. On the back of each strip write the sentence correctly.

"Hi Betsy," said Sue.

3. On twelve small tagboard squares make quotation marks.

4. Two or three players may play this game.

Player Directions:

1. Each player draws a sentence strip and four quotation
   mark cards.

2. On the count of three, the players place the quotation marks
   where they are needed.

3. Each player checks himself by turning the sentence strip
   over and reading the correct sentence.

4. The first person to place the quotation marks correctly
   wins and keeps the sentence strip.

5. Continue playing until all the strips have been used.

6. The player with the most strips wins.

VERB VARIETY

PURPOSE:

> After completing this activity, the student should be able to make sentences more interesting by changing the verbs.

Preparation Directions:

1. Enlarge the playing board below on tagboard to be used as a game board.

2. Provide markers for each player.

3. Two players may play this game.

Player Directions:

1. Each player chooses a marker and plays it on the board.

2. The first player moves one space and reads the verb. He must give a sentence using that verb, then substitute another verb for the same sentence. If he is unable to do this, he must move back one space.

3. Players continue to take turns until one player reaches Home.

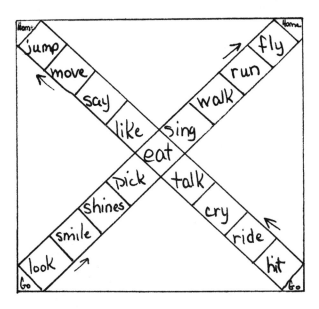

Notes

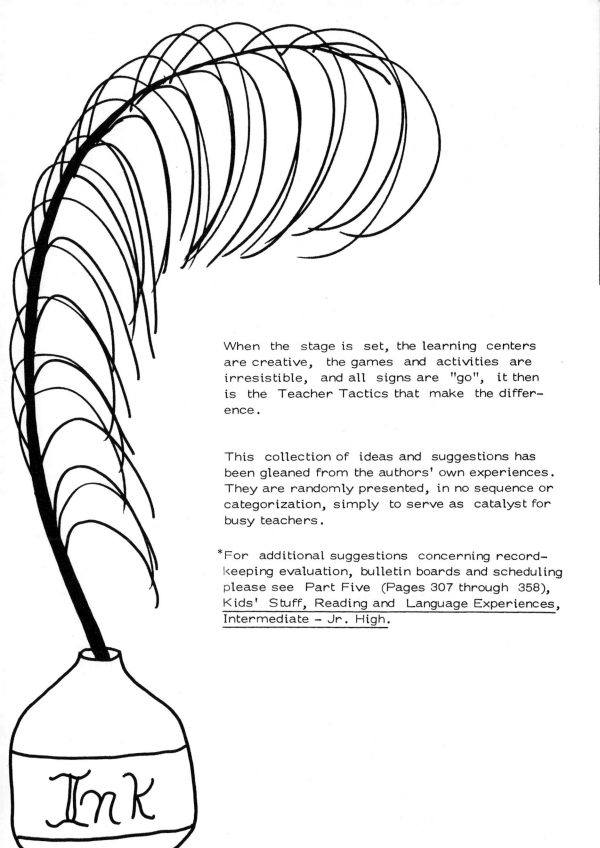

When the stage is set, the learning centers are creative, the games and activities are irresistible, and all signs are "go", it then is the Teacher Tactics that make the difference.

This collection of ideas and suggestions has been gleaned from the authors' own experiences. They are randomly presented, in no sequence or categorization, simply to serve as catalyst for busy teachers.

*For additional suggestions concerning record-keeping evaluation, bulletin boards and scheduling please see Part Five (Pages 307 through 358), Kids' Stuff, Reading and Language Experiences, Intermediate – Jr. High.

Students are highly sensitive to their teacher's creative efforts. Write stories, poems and plays, and devise creative charts and posters to share with your students. You'll be surprised at the joy and satisfaction you (and your students) derive from your own writing.

On a field trip to a brook, through a vacant lot or a wooded area ask students to select one thing to be brought back to the classroom and used as the object of a story or poem. A special corner can be arranged for sharing the poems and the objects that inspired them.

Help students to develop sensitivity to their natural surroundings by asking them to keep a diary for one week noting all the sounds they hear on their way to or from school, or to select one hour each day (preferably a different hour each day) and note all the different sounds they hear during that hour...

or by taking a nature walk in an area surrounding the school building, and while maintaining complete silence to make note of every sound heard.

Good books to read to students before these listening experiences
are: The Quiet Book by Helen M. Flynn, published by Wonder Books,
The Loudest Noise in the World by Benjamin Elkin, published by
Junior Literary Guild, and The Listening Walk by Paul Showers,
published by Crowell.

As one facet of vocabulary development, children will thrill to
exposure to sound words, color
words, movement words and feeling
words, presented on charts labeled
accordingly and written or illustrated
expressively.

Ask students to choose a favorite story or book and describe
verbally (in group discussion) the physical setting of the book or
story. Ask them to then design a travel folder to encourage tourists
to visit this place.

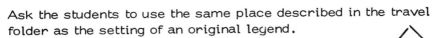

Ask the students to use the same place described in the travel
folder as the setting of an original legend.

Instruct students to select a favorite
story and write a different ending
for it. More mature students might
select a special book and rewrite
the last chapter. This experience
will be especially exciting if the
same stories or books are selected
by more than one student and the
surprise endings are compared
and/or contrasted.

Invite a local author of children's books to visit the class to discuss his work with the students. Guide students in advance planning so that questions concerning the author's goals, life style and own literary preferences are discussed. As a follow-up activity, students will profit from writing thank-you letters to the author with appropriate references to his works, as well as to the remarks made to the class.

A Beautiful Thought Box...

Turn a large shadow box picture frame into the "beautiful thought box" by lining it with red, black or purple velvet and providing pearl or rhinestone hat pins for pinning "beautiful thoughts" to

the background. Student nominations may be made for original poetry, stories or descriptive paragraphs to be displayed.

Consistent exposure to good poetry is the best way to instill in students a respect for and appreciation of the poetic form. Teachers will find that the time spent in selecting good poetry to share with students will pay large dividends in student interest in reading and writing poetry. The poem of the week might be printed on a large chart by the teacher and illustrated by a group of students...

or it might be dittoed by the teacher and copies distributed to all students to be illustrated and added to their own poetry booklet

...or it might be selected by a different student each week (from a collection made available by the teacher) and orally presented to the class and later printed on the chalk board to enable students to copy it for their booklets

... or it might be presented for choral reading one week, for pantomiming one week, and for dramatizing the next.

After sufficient poems for the booklet are collected, students should be given the guidance needed to organize and assemble them, complete an attractive cover and title page, and arrange the table of contents. (These booklets could make lovely Valentine or Mother's Day gifts.)

Utilize every opportunity for writing class letters and notes. Letters of inquiry, requests  for materials, invitations, acceptances and welcomes, thank you, get well and birthday notes can be meaningfully and creatively written.

Avoid dull and routine letter writing by asking students to write letters only when they have a reason that is real to them by leading a class discussion of the purpose of the letter and its implications, and by making a special vocabulary list that will encourage more expressive writing.

Assemble a collection of commonplace inanimate objects in a box labeled "Things to Think On". Ask students to go through the box until they find one thing they would like to take out to write about. Ask them to first write a paragraph (or paragraphs) describing the article and its use, to read their paragraph and put it aside.

...Ask them to then add the word "Magic" to the title and write a description of the article and its use. The clock that becomes a magic clock will certainly enable students to differentiate between the satisfaction of writing a descriptive paragraph and the joy of writing a creatively fanciful one.

Introduce word imagery to students by asking them to look for combinations of words that help them to "see" the author's intent and "feel" his purposes in selected passages from text and trade books used in the classroom. Encourage them to then evaluate their own writing in terms of transferring "imagery" to their readers through the use of colorful words and phrases.

Remind students to add interest to their writing by using different types of sentences.

Breathing fire, the warty green dragon...

Stress awareness of sentences that ask, order or show forceful emotions, as well as the more commonly used declarative sentences. They may be done in a directed teaching session involving paragraph writing using all four types of sentences. This would afford opportunity, too, to direct attention to proper punctuation for each type of sentence.

The move away from declarative sentences can be hastened by asking students to write sentences using "starters" designed to overcome the subject initiated sentence. The following list might be used:

Last night...
In spite of the snow...
Suddenly...
Fast and furiously...
Yesterday...
The other...
Before sunrise...
Over the mountain...

Excitement can be added to creative writing when students allow adjectives to follow the nouns they modify, such as

The dawn, cold and glistening, broke through the eerie suspense

rather than

The cold and glistening dawn broke through the eerie suspense.

Instruct students to put their heads down, close their eyes, and pretend their desk is a jet plane transporting them to the land of their dreams. Let them "dream awhile", then raise heads and open eyes to find paper and pencils on their desks to use to write the story of their adventuresome trip. This will be lots more fun when the teacher shares a dream trip too!

After a creative writing time, ask students to list all the words they used for the first time, all the words they could have substituted a more interesting word for, and all the words they use a lot but really "feel" to be expressive.

Invite each student to write his own autobiography. Stress honesty, accuracy and clarity while encouraging word usage to interest others. After auto-biographies are completed, ask students to exchange autobiographies to be used by other students as the basis for writing biographies. This activity should be preceded by a well-planned study on autobiographies and biographies appropriate to the age and interest level of the students.

Gathering information from reference and textbooks to use to write a biography of the composer of a favorite musical selection may be just the motivation some students need to "get into" biographies.

Students will enjoy working together in small groups to compile a biographical reference book. As they read biographies from the library, four or five-sentence entries, including important details of the person's life, may be written to be added to the reference book in alphabetical order.

Writing a sequel to a book read is an activity that will delight many students. They may want to work in pairs or in a small group to do this.

Instruct students to select a favorite character from a story or book. Ask them to pretend they are a newspaper reporter assigned to interview this character on a visit to their town today. Ask them to first prepare a list of questions they would want to ask this character, then write the story of the interview for their paper based on the questions asked. Provide time and opportunity for students to share their stories.

Instruct students to use a reference book (their social studies text, National Geographic magazine, encyclopedia, etc.) to find a city or country that interests them. Ask them to read about the place (some students will want to use more than one reference) and locate enough actual information to allow them to use it as the setting for an original story. Provide ample time and help for completion of stories and encourage sharing.

Prepare a story to be distributed to students. Ask them to select sentences from the story that portray one character as being sad, another happy, one frustrated, another excited, one surprised and another grateful. Instruct them to rewrite these sentences, using different adjectives but conveying the same general feeling. Provide time for students to read aloud and compare their sentences. A chart can be made listing all the words that convey the same feeling.

Instruct students to select a favorite story character and draw a picture of him, with special attention to his attire. Ask them to design a "new" image for their story character by giving him an entirely different wardrobe.

They may enjoy writing a paragraph or explaining orally to other members of the group the rationale for the new image.

Better results can be expected when creative writing experiences are tied to very real experiences. A snowy day poem will be more creative if written after a frolic in a new fallen snow, or a story concerning life on the farm will be more descriptive and "alive" when a trip to the farm has been enjoyed. (This sounds so obvious we almost hesitate to include it here, but then we remember that with the pressures of an academically weighted schedule teachers sometimes find themselves "following" the curriculum guide or teacher's manual, rather than planning to allow themselves the freedom necessary to take advantage of the "teachable moment".

Remember to give students lots of freedom to make choices related to their own creative writing efforts. Don't box them in with artificial assignments. For example, following a study of the sea shore, this assignment:

"Tonight see if you can write a story, a poem, a song or draw a picture expressing a feeling about the sea shore. If you aren't able to create something you'd like to share with your classmates tomorrow, find a story, poem, song or picture related to the sea shore in a magazine or book and bring it to share."

would be better than this one:

"Now that we've finished our study of the sea shore, everybody write a poem for homework and bring it to share tomorrow."

Provide a large selection of records and ask students to select music to represent the mood of the story or poem they have written. As a buildup for this exercise the students may select music for a story read by the teacher.

To help students acquire awareness of sequence development, collect comics from the Sunday newspaper, cut them apart and ask students to rebuild the sequence but to create at least one frame of their own to replace one of the original ones. Blank paper cut to the exact size of the frames, drawing pencils and crayons will facilitate completion of this activity. Some students may enjoy working in groups to design their own comic strips with original characters.

Students' appreciation for favorite books, vocabulary development and attention to writing style will be heightened by encouraging them to

      ...write a letter recommending the book to a friend in another town

      ...make up a different ending for the story

      ...write a diary as the main character of the story might write it

      ...write a book review to be added to the bulletin board in the school library

      ...write their honest opinion of the book to be added to a card file kept in the reading corner to be referred to as students select books to read

      ...add new words from the book to a class dictionary

      ...make a series of illustrations to depict the book's main events

      ...rewrite the book as a picture book suitable for younger children.

Encourage vocabulary development by asking students to select three characters from a story or book they have just completed. Ask them to make a chart by drawing the characters at the top of the chart and listing at least six characteristics of the character underneath. Ask them to list in an adjacent column a word meaning the opposite of the descriptive words. More mature students might enjoy rewriting the story portraying the characters in the role cast by the opposite characteristics.

A classroom window can become a "season showcase" mirroring changes in nature to motivate young writers to express creatively observations of their environment. Frame the window with construction paper or tagboard, label it, and provide comfortable seating, pads, and pencils to encourage students to continue their

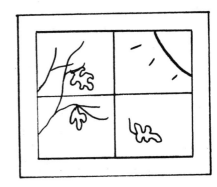

observations throughout the school year.

...An attractive bulletin board placed nearby to hold students' work will add interest and encourage sharing of ideas.

...Provide writing paper for this center that will fit into a loose leaf notebook. As papers are removed from the board they can be added to the anthology entitled "As Seen Through Our Window". By the end of the school year this anthology will present a complete picture of seasonal change and will be a source of pride to the student contributors. They might like to "will it" to next year's

students to give them a preview of "coming attractions".

Exposure to good books is the best approach to the development of plot and style. Plan to read to your students every day! Some good books to read aloud are:

Charlotte's Web – by E. B. White, Harper
Rabbit Hill – by Robert Lawson, Viking
Charlie and the Chocolate Factory –
Caddie Woodlawn – by Carol Brink, Little, Brown

Refer often to quotations from books read, and keep characters alive by giving them prominence in creative drama sessions. This will help students to develop appreciation of word usage and characterization and to see books as more than mere plot development.

Letters to main characters of books read will be fun for students to write. They may want to congratulate, condemn or argue with actions of the character. This would be a good activity to follow a book read aloud to the entire class. Students would enjoy seeing the differences in reactions within their group.

Prepare a bulletin board with the caption:

and suggestive first lines for stories, such as:

...what if the school bus failed to stop
...what if the snowman we built never melted
...what if the rug in our reading corner became a magic carpet to carry us
...what if the stuffed teddy bear suddenly came alive

Students will enjoy mounting their stories in the appropriate space on the board.

Ask students to state an opinion they hold on some currently controversial subject. Then use reference materials to gather at least three opinions held by different writers. Analyzing and summarizing the opinions gathered will provide a sound basis for comparing and contrasting for a written statement, including any revisions or reinforcements of the writer's original opinion.

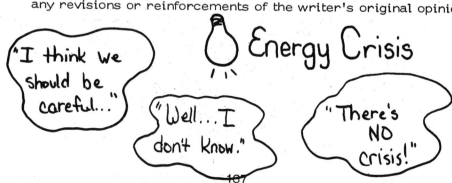

Plan and teach a good unit on the newspaper. Familiarity with all the features from the comics to the obituaries will help students develop appreciation for the total implications of the newspaper to daily living.

...Attention directed to differences in factual accounting of events and in feature stories will help students to develop awareness of style and plot presentation.

...Remind students that factual reporting should include information relating to

 Who? When? Where? Why?

...After reading a book or story, students will enjoy writing a feature news article (with a headline) telling the story as it might appear on the front page of the newspaper in the town where the story book place.

...As a culminating activity for this unit, publish a class newspaper. Even very young children will enjoy and profit from their assignment and the thrill of seeing their work in print in a real newspaper.

Plan directed teaching sessions to deal with similes and metaphors. Lead a group discussion and list ten of each on the chalk board, explaining the difference. Students might then like to make a chart for the writing center, using the following subheadings:

As round as a
   Sour ball...

He's a cool cat...

Similes Stated Comparisons	Metaphors Implied Comparisons

An excellent book for teachers to use to help children visualize and "feel" the excitement of color as expressed in words is Hailstones and Halibut Bones by Mary O'Neill, and illustrated by Leonard Weisgard, published by Doubleday and Company, Inc. After sharing this book some students will want to write their own color poems.

A table holding objects reflecting the "feel" of colors will stimulate originality and creativity; for example, a piece of purple velvet, a white lily, a red lipstick, an orange, a lump of black coal, a white cotton ball, etc.

Provide 3 x 5" cards for students to use to record six questions about a book they have just finished reading. These cards can be added to the collection in an attractively decorated box labeled "Six Questions" and placed with the book in the reading corner. They will serve as motivation for other  students to read the books. The back of the cards may be used by other students to record comments about the quality of the questions, or additional questions. As each student adds to the card and signs his name, the cards become more interesting to the entire group.

Load a large picnic basket with paperback books and place in a cozy corner of the classroom. Letter an attractive sign for the basket "Book-Nick! Pick-One!" Place no restrictions on when or for how long a book may be taken. Encourage students to read and share reactions to these books but refrain from making assignments or attaching teacher-structured academic objectives to this collection. Students who read "just for fun" are more prone to write "just for fun".

Provide art supplies for students to use to make posters advertising their original stories. These posters may be posted on the bulletin board to encourage other students to read the stories. In some instances students may wish to "swap-out" and illustrate each other's stories.

Encourage student awareness of descriptive words by supplying pictures of different objects and asking them to make a list of words that could be used to describe the object.

cat	rose	worm
fluffy	beautiful	slimy
fuzzy	pretty	slithery
cuddly	lovely	creepy
lively	gorgeous	crawly
snuggly	sweet	wiggly
wiggly	magnificent	

Help students to see how variety and interest can be achieved by varying the length of sentences. Write and/or read model paragraphs with two- and three-word sentences used in conjunction with sentences containing five, six, seven or more words.

As students' creative writing is checked, be on the lookout for unusual wording, highly descriptive phrases, or other exciting expressions. Make a chart listing these and giving credit to the author.

> **Telling It Well**
>
> The clouds floated lazily in the sky...(Susan)
>
> As gentle as a mother with her newborn babe...(Tom)

Writing letters to authors of favorite books is an activity that will "personalize" authors and help students to see them as real people. Many times these letters mailed in care of the publisher will be answered by the author.

Two books that will be of interest to teachers interested in children's creative writing are:

Miracles, Poems by Children of the English-Speaking World, by Richard Lewis, published by Simon and Schuster

Journeys, Prose by Children of the English-Speaking World, by Richard Lewis, published by Simon and Schuster

Make a collection of scenic pictures from magazines, travel posters and/or old calendars. Place them in the writing center for students to use in a variety of ways. They might want to:

...make a list of descriptive color words for each picture, using more expressive words such as golden, scarlet, topaz, jade, etc., rather than the ones more ordinarily used.

...write a story or a poem about the picture.

...draw at least three people or animals that could inhabit the scenic setting and write a story telling about their lives.

Ask students to put their heads on their desks and close their eyes while listening to records selected to invoke creative thinking and development of harmonious imagery. As the record is played a second time they will enjoy expressing their thoughts in a poem or a descriptive paragraph.

A good record to use for this activity is Tchaikovsky's Nutcracker Suite, directed by Leonard Bernstein, and distributed by Columbia.

Or they might enjoy making a scribble drawing during the first listening session and writing about what they see in the drawing as they listen the second time. A good record to use in this manner is Haydn's Surprise Symphony played by the Boston Pops and distributed by Columbia.

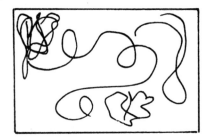

Provide experiences in plot development by starting a round-robin story and allowing students to take turns contributing to it.

Use flannel boards with felt figures or objects to start original stories. Provide additional felt objects for students to use to "get into" the story at strategic points. Keep the story going until all the children have had time to participate.

Some good sources for "read aloud" poems are:

Time for Poetry, by May Hill Arbothnot, published by
Scott Foresman

Sing A Song of Seasons, by John and Sara Brewton,
published by MacMillan

Teachers can have a positive role in helping children to evaluate
their own work. Using a separate piece of paper which can be
paperclipped to the original work, notes concerning the strong
points and suggestions for corrections or improvements can be
made. We prefer to never red pencil a student's creative efforts.

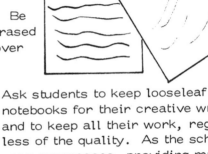

An acetate overlay placed over the
student's work and used for teachers'
remarks is an excellent aid to
teacher-student communication. Be
sure to use pencils that can be erased
so that the overlay can be used over
and over.

Ask students to keep looseleaf
notebooks for their creative writing
and to keep all their work, regard-
less of the quality. As the school
year progresses, providing many
opportunities for additions to be
made to the notebook, the young
authors will be impressed with the
improvement they are able to see
in their own writing style.

Provide a list of topics of current interest (these may range
from seasonal topics to political issues) and ask students to
select one to use as the subject of a magazine article. Before
beginning their own writing they will want to review articles
in numerous magazines for form and presentation. Remind
them that the "message" of their article will be made more
interesting by a tantalizing introduction and a climatic conclusion.

Play some lullabies to students and then ask them to write their
own. The soothing feeling of warmth and love that comes from
listening to lullabies provides the security base that will often
encourage the creative expression of personal feelings.

Fanciful and colorfully presented filmed stories will help boys and girls to develop mental imagery that will be transferable to their own writing. Two good ones are:

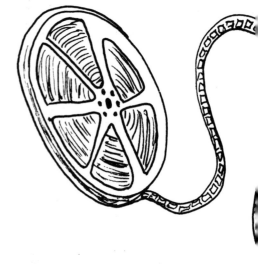

The Rolling Rice Ball
(a Japanese fairy tale)

and

The Musicians in The Woods
(animated puppets)

both distributed by Cornette Films.

Either of these films can be used as open-ended stories allowing students to view the first two-thirds and create their own ending. They will then enjoy comparing their version with their classmates and with the original.

To stimulate imagination and provide opportunity for experience in composing, record on tape a series of isolated sounds. Space these sounds at various intervals on the tape to enable students to listen to them and imagine them as the auditory part of an original story. Sounds might include humming, screeching, sobbing, grinding, clanking, laughing, clapping, etc. Students might enjoy listening to the tape in small groups and making up a group story to be written and illustrated. A collection of stories of this nature might be bound into a book for the reading table.

Students' original writing may be bound for the library or class-room reading corner by following this simple procedure:

Cut two pieces of card-
board for the front and
back covers of the book
and place on a flat surface,
leaving about three or
four inches of space between.

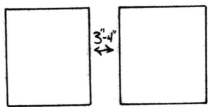

Tear heavy duty masking
tape into small pieces
and stick them on the
inside edges of the book
covers. Then turn the
covers over and do the
same thing on the other
side.

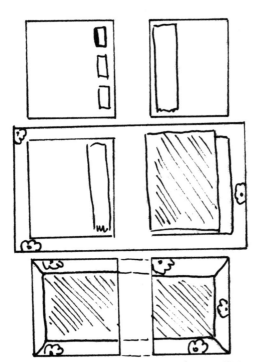

Next put one large piece
of masking tape down
the center of the tape.
Repeat this procedure
on both sides.

Cut contact paper to
extend beyond the sides,
and construction paper
in a complementary color
to fit the inside covers.
Then fold the contact
paper over the edges of
the covers so that the
construction paper is "stuck" to the cardboard by the contact paper
edges.

Punch holes in the sides of the covers and the pages of the completed
story. Use twisted yarn or cord to lace the book together.

The book's title and author may be
attractively lettered on the cover
with contrasting ink or letters may
be cut from solid colored construction or contact paper.

Notes

SELECTED REFERENCES

Applegate, Mauree, *Easy in English*, Chapters Two, Eight, and Twelve. New York: Harper and Row, 1960.

Applegate, Mauree, *Freeing Children to Write*. New York: Harper and Row, 1963.

Applegate, Mauree, *Helping Children Write*. Evanston, Ill.: Row, Peterson, 1954.

Arnstein, Flora J., *Children Write Poetry: A Creative Approach*. New York: Dover, 1967.

Arnstein, Flora J., *Poetry in the Elementary Classroom*. New York: Appleton Century Crofts, 1962.

Burrows, Alvina T., June D. Ferbee, Doris C. Jackson and Dorothy O. Saunders, *They All Want to Write*. Englewood Cliffs, New Jersey: Prentice-Hall, 1962.

*Forte, Imogene, Mary Ann Pangle and Robbie Tupa, *Center Stuff for Nooks, Crannies and Corners, Complete Learning Centers for Elementary Classrooms*. Nashville, Tennessee: Incentive Publications, 1973.

Forte, Imogene, Marjorie Frank and Joy MacKenzie, *Kids' Stuff, Reading and Language Experiences, Intermediate - Jr. High*. Nashville, Tennessee: Incentive Publications, 1973.

Forte, Imogene and Joy MacKenzie, *Nooks, Crannies and Corners, Learning Centers for Creative Classrooms*. Nashville, Tennessee: Incentive Publications, 1972.

Hughes, Ted, *Poetry Is*. New York: Doubleday and Company, 1970.

Koch, Kenneth, *Wishes, Lies and Dreams, Teaching Children To Write Poetry*. New York: Vantage Books, 1970.

Larrick, Nancy, *Somebody Turned On a Top in These Kids, Poetry and Young People Today*. New York: Delacorte Press, 1971.

Myers, R. E. and E. Paul Torrance, *Can You Imagine?* Boston: Ginn and Co., 1965.

Parnes, Sidney J. and Harold F. Harding (Editors), A Source
Book for Creative Thinking, Part Two, The Creative Process –
Philosophy and Psychology of Creativity. New York: Charles
Scribner's Sons, 1962.

Petty, Walter T. and Mary Bowen, Slithery Snakes and Other
Aids to Children's Writing. New York: Appleton Century
Crofts, 1967.

Petty, Walter T., Dorothy C. Petty, and Marjorie F. Becking,
Experiences in Language, Chapter Eight, Teaching Written
Expression. Boston: Allyn and Bacon, Inc., 1973.

Ross, Ramon R., Storyteller. Columbus, Ohio: Charles E.
Merrill, 1972.

Smith, James A., Creative Teaching of the Language Arts in
the Elementary School (Second Edition, Chapter Six). Boston:
Allyn and Bacon, Inc., 1973.

Torrance, E. Paul and R. E. Myers, Creative Learning and
Teaching. New York: Dodd, Mead and Company, 1970.

Walter, Nina Willis, Let Them Write Poetry. New York: Holt,
Rinehart and Winston, 1962.

Zirbes, Laura, Spurs to Creative Teaching. New York: Putnam,
1959.

*Please consult selected references (pages 374 and 375) in Center
Stuff for additional sources related to open education and the use
of learning centers.

Beautiful Thoughts

Bon Voyage
1. Select a sticker
2. Write a story
3. Illustrate your story adventure

Notes

Notes

Notes

Notes

Notes